Celebrating Diversity

Related Titles of Interest

Multicultural Education: Issues and Perspectives, Second Edition
James A. Banks and Cherry A. McGee Banks (Editors)
ISBN: 0-205-14044-0

Multiethnic Education: Theory and Practice, Third Edition
James A. Banks
ISBN: 0-205-14745-3

Teaching Strategies for Ethnic Studies, Fifth Edition
James A. Banks
ISBN: 0-205-12756-8

Comprehensive Multicultural Education: Theory and Practice, Second Edition
Christine I. Bennett
ISBN: 0-205-12181-9

101 Ways to Develop Student Self-Esteem and Responsibility Volume I: The Teacher as Coach
Jack Canfield and Frank Siccone
ISBN: 0-205-13368-1 Paper   0-205-13370-3 Cloth

100 Ways to Enhance Self-Concept in the Classroom, Second Edition
Jack Canfield and Harold Clive Wells
ISBN: 0-205-15415-8 Paper   0-205-15711-4 Cloth

101 Ways to Develop Student Self-Esteem and Responsibility Volume II: The Power to Succeed in School and Beyond
Frank Siccone and Jack Canfield
ISBN: 0-205-14068-8 Paper   0-205-14067-X Cloth

Multicultural Teaching: A Handbook of Activities, Information, and Resources, Third Edition
Pamela L. Tiedt and Iris M. Tiedt
ISBN: 0-205-12214-0

Celebrating Diversity

Building Self-Esteem in Today's Multicultural Classrooms

Frank Siccone
Siccone Institute, San Francisco

Allyn and Bacon
Boston • London • Toronto • Sydney • Tokyo • Singapore

Copyright © 1995 by Allyn and Bacon
A Division of Paramount Publishing
160 Gould Street
Needham Heights, Massachusetts 02194

Library of Congress Cataloging-in-Publication Data

Siccone, Frank
    Celebrating diversity : building self-esteem in today's
multicultural classrooms / Frank Siccone.
        p.   cm.
    Includes bibliographical references.
    ISBN 0–205–16390–4   0–205–16175–8 (pbk)
    1. Multicultural education—United States.   2. Self-esteem—Study
and teaching—United States.   3. Classroom management—United
States.   I. Title.
LC1099.S52 1995
370.19'6'0973—dc20   94-2727
                                                                             CIP

Printed in the United States of America

10 9 8 7 6 5 4 3 2 1 98 97 96 95 94

Dedication

To two generations of women in my family:

My mother, an infinite reservoir of love and compassion. One of the world's unsung heroines;

And my youngest niece and grandnieces: Sagina, Alex, and Jackie. May my vision for this book be realized if only a little so that the world you inherit will know better how to live in harmony.

*That our songs are different
is nowhere near as important
as the fact that
we all have a song to sing.*

—Frank Siccone

Contents

Introduction

To become moral communities that are supportive and caring, schools need to model empathy, altruism, trust, cooperation, fairness, justice, compassion, democracy, and celebration of diversity.
—Gerald J. Pine and Asa G. Hilliard III,
Rx for Racism: Imperatives for America's Schools

Not Just Tolerate. Celebrate!

Only about 3 percent of Americans can claim to be truly native (American Indians, Eskimos, Aleutian Islanders, and Hawaiians). All the rest of us are either immigrants or descendants of immigrants. Ethnic and cultural diversity is not new, and as a nation we will continue to become more and more diverse. Estimates are that by the year 2000, over a third of students nationwide will be from an ethnic minority.[1] Already in some states such as California, New Mexico, and Texas, Caucasian children make up less than 50 percent of the population. Minority students are now the majority.

This ever-increasing diversity among students is forcing a major restructuring of public education in the United States. The changes that are occurring are likely to transform the face of schools forever.

Public schools in the United States were originally designed for a homogeneous group of children with a common culture, common values, morals, ambitions, parental expectations, and so forth. Following the model of the Industrial Age, knowledge was broken down into its most elementary parts and schoolwork was done in assembly-line fashion. All that was required was a group of industrious students who were prompt, quiet, and obedient as they learned each isolated fact. Teachers took on the role of foreman, supervising the work and threatening expulsion—the equivalent of being fired—to those bold enough to challenge the system.

This approach to school was consistent with the overall approach to socialization usually referred to as the "melting pot." Individuals were thrown into the mix and their differences were "boiled away" as they were molded into true-blue Americans, living the "American way" and realizing the "American dream."

The dream, however, proved elusive for some and too expensive for others. The cost of giving up one's cultural identity in exchange for what often amounted to second-class citizenship was too big a price to pay. For others, this assimilationist dream was forbidden. The U.S. society that made it a crime to teach black slaves to read understood that literacy is the first step toward liberation. The society that perpetrated the full-scale internment of Japanese Americans—and not German or Italian Americans—made it clear that some cultures were not able or allowed to assimilate.

Some have suggested that the image of the "melting pot" be discarded for that of the "tossed salad." This new metaphor for cultural diversity recognizes that each group has its distinctive qualities to be valued and that different people can come together in a way that creates a new whole—one that reflects the integrity of the individual parts.

The issue isn't whether the United States will be a society made up of many cultures. It always has been and is becoming even more so. The issue is whether we will create a new vision for how our multicultural society will function effectively. In the absence of this new vision, we may be facing the Balkanization of America, with worsening racial conflicts similar to those of other countries that are divided into groups who are fighting for their ethnic identity and lack any sense of national identity.

It is a matter of America's self-image—our collective self-esteem.

Who we are in terms of our core values hasn't changed. "With liberty and justice for all," the right to "life, liberty, and the pursuit of happiness"—these remain as vital as ever. Martin Luther King, Jr., clearly understood the United States' moral vision as a country committed to the principle of liberty when he wrote from a jail cell: "We will reach the goal of freedom in Birmingham and all over the nation, because the goal of America is freedom. Abused and scorned though we may be, our destiny is tied up with America's destiny."[2]

Our challenge is to translate these values into practical reality for today's Americans. The issue is how to deal with both dimensions of the nation's motto; *E pluribus unum*—"Out of many, one."[3]

> *A*merica's dilemma has been our resistance to ourselves—our denial of our immensely varied selves. But we have nothing to fear but our fear of our own diversity.
> —Ronald Takaki

Schools have a crucial role to play in helping to create a society that includes everyone, one that not only tolerates but celebrates diversity. As with the rainbow—another metaphor used in this context—where each color reflects light in its own way and contributes to the overall beauty of the phenomenon, so, too, all the colors of the human race illuminate the magnificence of the human experience.

Multicultural education not only supports the long-range goal of transforming society, it also serves the more immediate objective of transforming schools.

It is providing a real opportunity to develop educational methodologies that work for all students. I believe that all good education is student-centered. Teaching strategies such as individualized instruction, learning centers, experience-based learning, and cooperative learning are transforming classrooms from traditional teacher-directed lecture formats to student-centered environments. The same strategies are recommended for multicultural classrooms. Effective practices for teaching in a multicultural setting are the same practices that characterize all good teaching.

Characteristics of Good Teachers

Based on teacher-effectiveness research,[4] the following practices have been identified as characteristics of good teachers. Teachers who are effective:

1. Believe that all their students are capable learners and expect that all children will achieve.

2. Assign tasks which provide realistic challenges.

3. Involve all students in learning activities wherever possible.

4. Monitor student progress by asking questions and circulating around the room.

5. Give adequate feedback so students know what they have learned and what skills need to be learned.

6. Use guiding and probing questions when students don't know the answers.

7. Direct questions to specific students rather than to those who volunteer.

8. Find ways to get students to cooperate with one another and take responsibility for their own work.

9. Minimize the time students spend doing independent seat-work.

10. Make sure that students master one unit or lesson before moving on to the next.

11. Are well organized and able to prevent management and instructional problems from occurring.

12. Encourage positive student behavior and handle inappropriate behavior with minimal negative affect.

13. Have more time for classroom academic tasks because classroom routines have been minimized.

14. Give uninterrupted, focused instructional activities to students.

15. Have appropriate presentation skills to explain, demonstrate, and discuss.

Toward a Culture of Esteem

The purpose of this book is to give educators—teachers, administrators, counselors, instructional aides, resource staff, parents, and so forth—tools they can use to build self-esteem for all students in today's multicultural classrooms and schools.

Students who attend classes that are geared only to the majority culture—where no recognition is given to the legitimacy of other cultures—are likely to feel isolated and inferior. It should be no surprise that the students who tend to have the most difficulty in school (Native Americans, African Americans, and Hispanics) are from groups who have experienced a long history of subjugation, prejudice, and discrimination.[5] What happens to a child when—as Adrienne Rich expresses it—"someone with the authority of a teacher" presents a portrait of America, and "you are not in it"? . . . "a moment of psychic disequilibrium, as if you looked into a mirror and saw nothing."[6]

> *We need to consider the role that schools and society in general have in creating low self-esteem in children. That is, students do not simply develop poor self-concepts out of the blue. Rather they are the result of policies and practices of schools and society that respect and affirm some groups while devaluing and rejecting others.*
> —Sonia Nieto

In order for children to develop a healthy sense of self, they need to experience themselves as unique individuals who are accepted for who they are. They also need to feel that they belong, that they are important members of their families, their circle of friends, and their communities. This can only really occur in a multicultural, bias-free, antiracist environment that sincerely values all people of all cultures equally.

Multicultural education is more than just adding references about other cultures to the existing mainstream-centric perspective. Adding Martin Luther King, Jr., to our list of heroes while leaving the rest of U.S. history unaltered is not sufficient. The very structure of the curriculum must be transformed so that events, issues and concepts are viewed from many different cultural perspectives—all of equal validity. Let's hear from Native Americans, for example, about how Columbus "discovered" America.

In order for students to function effectively in today's complex world, they need to understand that life does not translate easily into multiple-choice questions. The answers to the important problems in life cannot always be found in the back of the book.

A multicultural approach encourages the development of critical thinking skills in students by providing a diversity of values and many different perspectives from which to interpret events. Students are challenged to seek their own answers rather than simply memorize and recite those of the teacher or of the predominant culture.

> *I*t is a waste of time hating a mirror
> or its reflection
> instead of stopping the hand
> that makes glass with distortions.
>
> —Audre Lorde

It is helpful to define culture as not only the artifacts, customs, heritage and traditions of a group but also their values and way of interpreting the world. In this sense, culture is how a social group survives in and adapts to its environments—natural, social, and metaphysical.[7]

Can you imagine Polynesian culture existing anywhere except in the tropics? Could Impressionistic painting have originated anywhere but in France, or Andy Warhol anywhere but in the United States during the 1960s and 1970s? Soul music and the blues could only have been born in Black America, and the physical and metaphysical realities of Native Americans were clearly intertwined.

The dynamic interplay between people and their various environments is also a critical concept in the understanding of self-esteem. Nathaniel Branden defines *self-esteem* as "the disposition to experience onself as competent to cope with the challenges of life and as deserving of happiness"—in essence, *self-respect* and *self-efficacy*.[8]

Learning how social groups have survived in and adapted to their physical, social, and metaphysical environments (i.e., the challenges of life), then, is an aim of multicultural education; and an aim of self-esteem education is to experience oneself as competent to do the same.

Critics of self-esteem education in schools confuse it with "touchy-feely," happy-face pollyannaism that takes time away from the teaching of basic skills. In fact, self-esteem is the most basic of skills. Some argue that self-esteem is the result of achievement rather than a precursor to it. In my view, this is really a chicken-and-egg situation. It takes a certain degree of self-esteem to envision the possibility that I could succeed at something and to have the confidence necessary to risk the attempt. The resulting success, in turn, builds my self-esteem and promotes the likelihood of future achievement.

Self-esteem involves an interactive relationship between oneself and one's environment. What I believe about myself determines how I relate to others. Their feedback, in turn, affects how I feel about myself, and so forth.

One way of conceptualizing the dynamics involved is to relate the one dimension of self/other to the other dimension of internal/external and diagram it as follows:

	Experience (Internal)	Express (External)
Others	Interdependence 2.	Social Responsibility 4.
Self	Independence 1.	Personal Responsibility 3.

Quadrant 1 (Part I of this book) is focused on the internal experience of self-worth that includes a recognition of oneself as an independent, autonomous being who is unique in all the world. Issues of *identity* are dealt with: Who am I? What makes me me? What makes me special?

Quadrant 2 (Part II) is involved with the experience of our interdependence. In order for our schools, our communities, our society, our world to be truly functional, everyone must be valued. This section is related to the need to *belong*: connectedness, affiliation, and friendship.

Quadrant 3 (Part III) is related to personal responsibility, which is a logical expression of self-esteem. This section is designed to help students increase their sense of *power* to control their lives and expand their ability to be successful. Achievement, purposefulness, self-directedness, risk taking, and goal attainment are all part of this.

Quadrant 4 (Part IV), *social responsibility,* is intended to encourage students to move beyond personal self-interest to accepting greater responsibility for the world around them. Activities are included to develop students' social and interpersonal skills, which are becoming increasingly important as more and more schools use cooperative learning methods and as a growing number of businesses are using work teams to improve productivity.

The second half of this final section is devoted to the significant role that *contribution* and service play in people's experience of happiness and self-worth. I believe that every human being has as his or her purpose the desire to make a difference—a positive difference expressed in some unique way. Related to our metaphysical environment, it is a way of finding meaning for our existence.

Children who accept themselves as worthwhile are more likely to accept and value others. Children who have confidence in themselves are more apt to participate actively, take greater risks, and find new ways to overcome obstacles to their success. Children who feel included as valued members of society are less likely to vandalize it. Children who feel capable of living meaningful lives are less likely to waste theirs.

Celebrating diversity is not only the right thing to do because it is consistent with our nation's core values, it is also the smart thing to do because it offers the best chance of working—and pragmatism has always been an important characteristic of America's culture.

> *No one has yet fully realized the wealth of sympathy, kindness and generosity hidden in the soul of a child. The effort of every true education should be to unlock that treasure.*
>
> —Emma Goldman

Now for the Most Important Variable—YOU

> *Modeling is not the best way to teach. It is the only way to teach.*
>
> —Albert Schweitzer

Research indicates that students pick up on teachers' attitudes even when the teacher is unaware of having negative feelings.

You can't teach what you don't know, and you can't give what you don't have.

Your own feelings of self-worth, self-respect, and self-efficacy are essential to your ability to support your students in building their self-esteem. Likewise, your attitudes about other races and ethnic groups as well as your own cultural heritage are critical to your creating a classroom environment that celebrates diversity.

In essence, you must become a multicultural person,[9] which involves an appreciation for learning as a lifelong process, an openness to viewing things from various perspectives, a willingness to confront your own prejudices, and a commitment to esteeming yourself and others—all others.

It is strongly recommended that you do all the activities in this book yourself before using them with your students so that you experience them as a participant and have the opportunity to process any issues that arise for yourself.

When conducting the activities with students, it is important that you take an active role—demonstrating an appropriate level of self-disclosure, risk-taking, and enthusiasm for the process.

The activities are not intended to be done in isolation. Rather, they are meant to serve as catalysts for creating an inclusive and esteeming environment that is ongoing. Respect for self and others does not end when the activity is over.

You are welcome to do the activities in sequence or pick and choose the ones that are most appropriate for you and your students. Not all the activities are suitable for all grade levels. Those requiring a lot of writing or the analysis of complex feelings would need to be simplified when being used with younger children.

Some of the activities can be done in a few minutes at the beginning or end of the day, or when you want to change the energy level in the classroom. Many of the exercises will take the equivalent of a full class period, and a few could be extended over a period of days or weeks.

As much as possible, integrate the material into your regular routine. "Promises to Keep" (Activity 27), "My Circle of Friends" (Activity 28), and "Let There Be Peace on Earth: Conflict Management" (Activity 63) could be used as part of your classroom management program.

"Multicultural Support Teams" (Activity 30), "SHARE to Show You Care" (Activity 57), and "Team Problem Solving" (Activity 61) could be used in conjunction with cooperative learning.

A number of the lessons could serve as the focus of a theme-based unit of study to which all academic subjects could be related. "The Joy of Eating" (Activity 21), "The Cultures We Are" (Activity 23), and "Community Service Projects" (Activity 69) are some examples.

Children learn not just by what they are told, but also by what they see and feel for themselves. The more aspects of the school environment that are involved, the more successful any program will be. Diversity needs to be celebrated not only in the formal curriculum but also in the "covert curriculum." The values, attitudes, beliefs, and actions of staff and students; school policies and politics; teaching and learning styles; assessment procedures; and community involvement all teach very clear lessons. Perhaps you could enlist the support of your colleagues in adapting the activities in this book into a schoolwide program.

My purpose in writing this book is to contribute to you, and I am certain that your purpose in reading it is to contribute to your students. I trust that, in turn, your students will be inspired by a new vision of what is possible for them: a vision where everyone is included, everyone is valued, everyone is successful, and everyone contributes.

Notes

1. Ana Consuelo Matiella, *Positively Different: Creating a Bias-Free Environment for Young Children* (Santa Cruz, CA: Network Publications, 1991), p. 2.

2. Martin Luther King, *Why We Can't Wait* (New York: New American Library, 1964), pp. 92–93.

3. Ronald Takaki, *A Different Mirror: A History of*

Multicultural America (Boston: Little, Brown, 1993), p. 3.

4. Barbara Larrivie, *Strategies for Effective Classroom Management* (Boston: Allyn and Bacon, 1992), p. 461.

5. Jim Cummins, *Empowering Minority Students* (Sacramento: California Association of Bilingual Education, 1989), p. 8.

6. Adrienne Rich, *Blood, Bread and Poetry: Selected Prose, 1979–1985* (New York: Norton, 1986), p. 199.

7. Brian M. Bullivant, "Culture: Its Nature and Meaning for Educators," in *Multicultural Education: Issues and Perspectives,* ed. James A. Banks and Cherry A. McGee Banks (Boston: Allyn and Bacon, 1989), pp. 28–29.

8. Nathaniel Brandon, *The Power of Self-Esteem* (Deerfield Beach, FL: Health Communications, Inc., 1992), pp. 17–20.

9. Sonia Nieto, *Affirming Diversity: The Sociopolitical Context of Multicultural Education* (White Plains, NY: Longman, 1992), p. 275.

Acknowledgments

I am truly blessed and deeply grateful to the many people who have contributed to my happiness and success.

For support with this book I am indebted to the following people:

- Dorothy Divack for her creative input and administrative coordination

- Robert Wright for doing an outstanding job with research assistance, manuscript preparation, and a zillion other things

- Jessica Brindle, Kathy Shean, and Richard Wixo for helping with research and David Nottage for his assistance with manuscript preparation

- Dr. Lulu Lopez, Baldwin Park Unified School District; Dr. Kathryn Weed, California State University, San Bernardino; and Susan Whitten of the Ralph Wheelock School in Medfield, Massachusetts, for their excellent suggestions for improving the text

- My friends at Allyn and Bacon—Mylan Jaixen and Sue Hutchinson—for their encouragement and editorial wisdom

- Dr. Hanoch McCarty, whose recommendations enhanced the book considerably and whose friendship enhances my life considerably

- Chris Jehle for editing, proofreading, and contributing in many other ways throughout the process

Self-Esteem and Independence

Freedom to Be Me

*O*f every hue and caste am I,
I resist any thing better than my own diversity.
—Walt Whitman

	Experience (Internal)	Express (External)
Others	Interdependence	Social Responsibility
Self	Independence	Personal Responsibility

$$Chapter \quad 1$$

Identity
Who Am I?

*Nothing said to us, nothing we can learn from others,
reaches us so deep as that which we find in ourselves.*
—Theodore Reik

Introduction

*Be humble, for the worst thing in the world is of the
same stuff as you; be confident, for the stars are of the
same stuff as you.*
—Nicholai Velimirovic

*Amazing Grace.**

> She loved stories. Stories she read in books. Stories she saw in movies. Stories her grandmother told. Stories she made up herself.
>
> Grace would often act out the stories, taking the best part for herself, of course. She was Joan of Arc, Hiawatha, Aladdin. She healed the sick, sailed the seven seas, and experienced lost kingdoms.
>
> When her teacher said that the class was going to do the play, Peter Pan, Grace knew exactly who she wanted to be.
>
> "You can't be Peter", said one of her classmates, "that's a boy's name." And another said, "You can't be Peter Pan. He isn't black."

*Amazing Grace by Mary Hoffman, pictures by Caroline Binch (New York: Dial, 1991).

With some support from her mother and grandmother, Grace realized that she could do anything she wanted, if she put her mind to it.

Back at school on Monday, auditions were held to pick the best student for the part in the play.

Grace had been practicing being Peter Pan all weekend. She knew all the words to say and all the things to do. Everyone voted for Grace because her performance was truly amazing!

This first chapter is about belief in oneself. It is meant to bolster children's sense of independence, making it safe for them to be themselves in all their uniqueness and express themselves in all their wonderfulness.

1 The Name Game

*I am the one whose love
overcomes you, already with you
when you think to call my name.*

—Jane Kenyon

Background*

This first section of the book deals with one of the fundamental building blocks of self-esteem—a sense of identity. The experience of valuing myself is predicated on the awareness of myself as a distinct, unique individual.

Virtually all cultures provide for the need for self-identity by using names to distinguish one person from another, although the approach to naming may differ.

- Many children are named after a close relative or friend of the family. Sharing a name with someone can create a special bond.

- The day of birth is commonly used in Tibet as the source of a baby's name: Sunday, *Nyma*; Monday, *Dawa*; Tuesday, *Mingma*.

*The background information regarding naming customs from diverse cultures was found in *Mamatoto: A Celebration of Birth* by Carroll Dunham and The Body Shop Team (New York: Penguin Books, 1991).

- Names based on things in nature are used by the Miwok Indians of California: *iskemu,* water running gently when the creek dries; *kono,* a squirrel biting through the center of a pine nut.

- In Hawaii, an event that occurred at the time of birth often serves as the inspiration for a name. *Kapaulehuaonapalilahilahiokaala* means the lehua flower blooming on the step of ridges of Mount Kaala.

- People who believe in reincarnation seek to discover the child's true name. The Dyak of Borneo, for example, offer the baby a bundle of reeds with the names of ancestors inscribed on them. The one that the child touches is assumed to be the correct name.

Purpose

Since one significant aspect of our identity is our name, exploring the origins and significance of your students' names with them can help strengthen their sense of being unique.

This series of exercises will also increase students' appreciation for their own and other cultures, given that most names have associations with one's family, ethnic group, religion, and so forth.

The first activity is a good ice breaker on the first day of school in that it helps students remember each other's names in a way that is fun and exciting.

Procedure

1. Have students sit in a circle, or divide them into two or three circles of ten or so.

2. Introduce the activity as being a fun and easy way of learning each other's names.

3. Explain that each student will introduce him- or herself by first name and a word that describes how he or she is feeling this morning. The word is to begin with the same first letter or sound as the student's name to give an association that will help the others remember the student's name.

    Give examples such as:

    > "Hi, I'm **D**orothy and I'm **d**elighted to be here."
    > "Hi, I'm **K**ris and I feel **c**ool."
    > "Hi, I'm **A**lonzo and I'm **a**lert."

4. Start the process yourself or ask for a volunteer to begin. As you go clockwise around the circle, the second person first states the name

and adjective of the person to his or her right and then states his or her own name and descriptive word.

The third person repeats what the first and second students have said and so forth around the circle until the last person begins with the first person and continues around the circle, remembering each of the students' names and adjectives.

5. Students often get excited and tend to help out if the person whose turn it is has trouble remembering. We suggest that the student who is speaking be given a chance to do it on his or her own. If help is needed, he or she can request it.

6. At the end of the activity, allow the students to share their feelings about doing the exercise. You may also want to read them a book about names, *Adelaide to Zeke* by Janet Wolf (New York: Harper & Row, 1977).

Other books—selected for their thematic relevance to the activities—are listed at the back of each chapter. This section includes a number of stories of children whose names are clearly culture-specific. You may want to read one of these in conjunction with each of the activities in this chapter.

When reading books to your students, it is always helpful to hold the book up to show the pictures. Another way to have everyone see the pictures is to duplicate each page of the book onto an overhead transparency and show that transparency as you read that page in the book. Doing this will help hold the students' attention.

2 The Name Game—II

Purpose

This is essentially the same as Activity 1 with a slight variation. This activity works well on the second day to reinforce students' memories of each other's names.

It is also an opportunity for students to affirm a positive attribute or strength that they possess.

Procedure

1. Set up the exercise with students in a circle, the same as in Activity 1.

2. This time, when the students introduce themselves, they are to state a positive attribute, strength, talent, or skill that they have. A list of positive feeling words is provided for your reference. Once again, they are to use an adjective that starts with the same letter as their name. Give them some examples, such as:

   "Hi, I'm Dimitri and I **d**ance well."
   "Good morning, I'm Hanoch and I'm **h**onest."
   "I'm Essence and I'm **e**nergetic."

Positive Feeling Words

adorable	gorgeous	pleased
adoring	grateful	quick
beautiful	gratified	quiet
blissful	great	rapturous
calm	handsome	ravishing
celebrating	happy	rejoicing
centered	hilarious	relaxed
cheerful	honest	relishing
confident	intelligent	reveling
content	jolly	satisfied
delighted	joyous	serene
ecstatic	jubilant	soaring
elegant	kind	stunning
enchanted	lively	tender
energetic	lovely	thrilled
enjoying	loving	tranquil
enthusiastic	merry	triumphant
excellent	mirthful	understanding
excited	neat	vivacious
exhilarated	nice	wonderful
fun-loving	outrageous	yummy
fulfilled	overjoyed	zany
gentle	peaceful	
glad	pleasant	

Suggestion: Let the students brainstorm their own list of adjectives. They will come up with some amazing words. (Slang words should be accepted. If inappropriate language is suggested, use this as an opportunity to discuss what makes some words offensive, and ask the students to agree to use only words that are acceptable to everyone in the class.)

3 Name Toss

*A man who finds no satisfaction in himself,
seeks for it in vain elsewhere.*

—La Rochefoucauld

Purpose

This activity builds on the previous ones and can be used, again, to help students remember the names of their classmates. It is also an opportunity for the students to give and receive positive feedback from one another.

Materials

One of the following for each group of students:

basketball
soccer ball
pine cone
tennis ball
Frisbee
Koosh ball (available in rainbow colors)
heart-shaped beanbag

Procedure

1. This activity can be done outdoors as a physical education exercise with the students standing in a circle using a basketball, soccer ball, pine cone, tennis ball, or Frisbee. The smaller objects, a Koosh ball or a beanbag, can be used if the activity is done in the classroom with the students seated in a circle. You can divide the class into groups of around ten students per group or keep the entire class together.

2. Describe the activity and then begin it yourself or ask for a volunteer.

3. The first person calls out the name of someone else in the circle and says something positive about him or her—something he or she likes or admires about this other student—while tossing the ball or object.

4. The student who receives the object, in turn, calls out the name and positive attribute of another while tossing the object to this next person.

5. The activity continues until everyone has been called. Each student can be called only once.

Only positive statements are allowed.

4 Name Flag

A man's name is not like a mantle which merely hangs about him, and which one perchance may safely twitch and pull, but a perfectly fitting garment, which, like the skin, has grown over him, at which one cannot rake and scrape without injuring the man himself.

—Goethe

Purpose

This is an art activity that will allow students to increase their sense of identity while linking their name with their country of origin.

Materials

one piece of art paper for each student
crayons, colored marking pens, or paints

Procedure

1. Prior to the day of the activity, have students research the colors of the flag of their country of origin.

Encourage them to trace their ancestry back to another country and find a picture of the country's flag to discover what colors are used.

In cases where students' families have immigrated from more than one country, students could pick the one with which they most identify, or the one that is least common, or the one they like the best.

If some students don't know what colors to use or don't want to use the colors of their country's flag, they could choose colors that are important to them.

2. Hand out the art supplies and ask the students to write or print their name on the page as large as possible.

3. Next have them draw random lines over the page to create an abstract design.

4. Now instruct them to color in each space using one of the colors of their country's flag. Each adjoining space should be a different color.

5. Let students hang their flags on a bulletin board in the classroom or in one of the school's corridors.

   Ask the students to explain their designs, the colors used, what makes them unique, and so forth.

6. Discuss with your students what they learned from doing the activity. Encourage students to discover the symbolism of the colors and designs used in their country's flags.

5 Let Your Fingers Do the Talking

The highest result of education is tolerance.

—Helen Keller

Purpose

By learning their name in another language—Braille—students will have another opportunity to strengthen their sense of identity while learning something about their visually handicapped peers.

Procedure

1. Begin by asking your students a series of questions, such as:

   "How many of you know someone who is blind or visually handicapped?"

   "Do you know how people who are not sighted read and write?"

   "How many of you know what Braille is?"

   "Where have you seen Braille used?" (Some elevators and ATM machines have Braille instructions posted.)

2. Let your students know that today they are going to learn how to write their names in Braille. Hand out copies of the Braille Alphabet Worksheet and the My Name in Braille Worksheet.*

3. Ask students to take the My Name in Braille Worksheet and print their first name in the top row of boxes, one letter in each box.

4. Then say, "Next look up each letter in the Braille alphabet and color in the appropriate dots in the box below each letter of your first name. Fill in each box until you have spelled out the letters in your name."

5. Have the students hold up their completed My Name in Braille Worksheets to share with their classmates.

Variation I

Since Braille is meant to be read with fingers, not eyes, you may want to give students a way of making their name in Braille tactile by having them glue split peas onto the circles that they colored in with pencil.

Variation II

The same activity could be done using any language. Languages based on a writing system different from the English alphabet—Hebrew, Japanese, and so forth—would be particularly interesting.

You could also teach your students how to use American Sign Language (ASL) to spell out their names.

*This activity is reprinted with permission from *Children of the Rainbow—First Grade* by the Board of Education of the City School District of the City of New York.

Braille Alphabet Worksheet

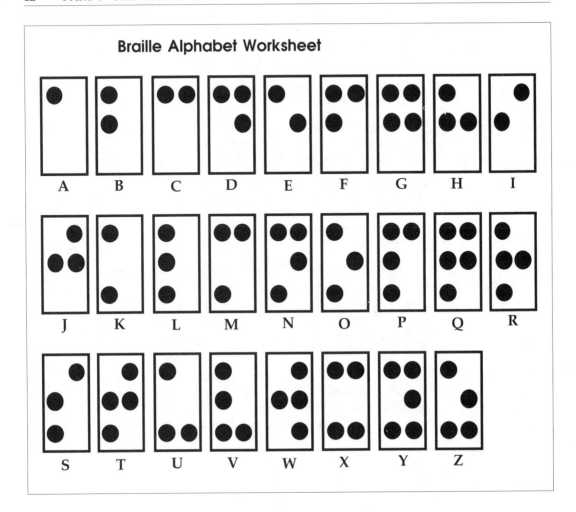

My Name in Braille Worksheet

○ ○	○ ○	○ ○	○ ○	○ ○	○ ○	○ ○	○ ○
○ ○	○ ○	○ ○	○ ○	○ ○	○ ○	○ ○	○ ○
○ ○	○ ○	○ ○	○ ○	○ ○	○ ○	○ ○	○ ○

○ ○	○ ○	○ ○	○ ○	○ ○	○ ○	○ ○	○ ○
○ ○	○ ○	○ ○	○ ○	○ ○	○ ○	○ ○	○ ○
○ ○	○ ○	○ ○	○ ○	○ ○	○ ○	○ ○	○ ○

6 Name Interviews

*Say
who I am.
Set
our two fires climbing.*
—Mary Virginia Micka

Purpose

For students to deepen their sense of identity by discussing the significance of their names, including their thoughts and feelings, family association, cultural connections, and so forth.

Procedure

1. Have students find a partner. Use a creative way of doing this—for example:

   "Find someone who is wearing the same color shoes as you are."

   "Line up according to birthday and pair up with the person whose birthday is closest to yours."

   "Find someone whose Name Flag has the same colors as yours."

   "Count the number of letters in your first name. If you have an even number of letters, find a partner whose name also has an even number. If your name has an odd number of letters, find a partner whose name has an odd number."

2. Instruct the students to take turns interviewing each other about their names. Whenever students are working in pairs, encourage them to sit facing each other to enhance their communication and sense of connection.

   You may hand out a copy of the Name Interview Worksheet to each pair of students, or put the questions on the board.

Note: In addition to or instead of the questions on the worksheet, you can let the students ask any other questions that they have about their partner's name. A good rule here is that students can ask any question they want, provided it is a question they would be willing to answer themselves. Also, students should always be given the option to pass.

3. Bring the students together to discuss what they learned about each other and about how people get named. You can structure this by having students introduce their partner, telling the class some interesting facts about their partner's name.

   Continue the discussion by focusing on cultural aspects of your students' names—for example:

   - The common practice in Spanish-speaking nations of using both the father's surname and the mother's maiden surname
   - The Vietnamese custom of putting the surname first, then the middle name, and the given name last
   - The movement among African Americans to confirm pride in their cultural heritage by using names from their homeland rather than names whose historical roots are traced back to the days of slavery
   - The tendency of third- and fourth-generation descendants of immigrants to have Americanized first names coupled with their traditional family surname

Name Interview Worksheet

1. What is your name?

2. How do you feel about your name? What do you like about it? What don't you like about it?

3. What do you know about how you got that name? Were you named after someone else? Who named you?

4. Are there members of your family who have the same name?

5. Do you have any classmates who have the same name as yours?

6. Are there any famous people who have the same name as yours?

7. In what ways are you like or not like these other people who have the same name?

8. Does your name have any other meaning?

9. Was your name originally in another language? How do you say it in the other language? What does your name mean in this other language?

10. If you could pick a different name, what name would you want?

11. What do you like about that name?

12. Native Americans often have names that describe something about them or compare them to something in nature—Whispering Elk, Sitting Bull, Running Deer. If you could make up such a name for yourself, what would it be?

7 Brand Names

What a man thinks of himself, that it is which determines or rather indicates his fate.

—Henry David Thoreau

Purpose

In our consumer-oriented economy, a considerable amount of effort goes into developing brand names for companies and their products. For everything from banks to soap detergents, advertising is used to create a brand personality that will entice people to buy or do business with them rather than with their competitors.

Companies work hard to create a corporate image and logo that is recognizable and instills confidence in the consumer who makes the decision to purchase this product.

This activity invites students to think of themselves as special and challenges them to translate their uniqueness into a visual image.

Materials

white paper (8½″ × 11″), one per student
crayon or colored markers or paints

Procedure

1. Hand out copies of the Brand Names Worksheet depicting logos from a number of community organizations and discuss.

   - What do they think the images are supposed to signify or remind them of?
   - What are their favorite foods, toys, clothes, places to eat, and so forth, and what logos do these companies use?

2. Hand out Brand Names Worksheet II and have the students use this to identify ways in which they are special that might then be used in their logo.

3. Distribute the art supplies and instruct the students to draw a logo that represents how they are unique and how they want others to think of them.

You may have the students work in small groups to share supplies and help each other think of things to draw.

You probably want to go around from student to student coaching them on their designs.

4. When the students are finished with their logo designs, have them share in small groups or as a full class, and post the drawings in the classroom or school.

Note: If you have the necessary equipment, the students could develop their logo using computer graphics.

Brand Names Worksheet I

HOSTELLING INTERNATIONAL

HOSTELLING INTERNATIONAL

Stressing the ideals of world peace and inter-cultural exchange, American Youth Hostels provides hostels for day and overnight trips, and environmental education programs.

The San Francisco SPCA

2500 16th STREET • SAN FRANCISCO, CA 94103

THE SAN FRANCISCO SPCA

The Society for the Prevention of Cruelty to Animals acts as an advocate on behalf of animals and as an enforcer of their rights.

CALIFORNIA ACADEMY OF SCIENCES

Through research and education, the Academy works to awaken wonder and inspire respect for the natural world.

ZEN HOSPICE PROJECT

ZEN HOSPICE PROJECT

The Zen Hospice Project is dedicated to bringing greater sensitivity and compassion in caring for people coping with life-threatening illness.

*Logos are used with permission from the respective organizations.

Brand Names Worksheet II

My favorite color is _____

My favorite shape is _____

My favorite subject in school is _____

My favorite sport/hobby is _____

My favorite food is _____

My favorite music is _____

What I like best about myself is _____

What I want others to remember about me is _____

It is in part the very uniqueness of every individual that makes him, not only a member of a family, race, nation or class, but a human being.
—Helen Merrel Lynd

8 A Sandwich by Any Other Name

Purpose

A hungry eighteenth-century nobleman requested a snack. The resulting concoction, consisting of two pieces of bread with a slice of meat between them, has become identified ever since with the Earl of Sandwich.

This is probably the most familiar example of an *eponym:* a word in common usage that was once the name of an actual person.

The purpose of this activity is for students to increase their sense of pride by considering how their names might live beyond them as a designation for something that people find useful.

Procedure

1. Hand out copies of the Eponym Worksheet* and have students connect the names in column 1 with the items in column 2.

    You may want to allow the students to work cooperatively in small groups to make the accurate identification of items. Dictionaries and encyclopedias may also be made available for students to research the items that are unknown to them. (Answers on page 23.)

2. Next, have the students consider something with which they might like to have their name connected. It may be something that does not yet exist that the student could imagine creating, or something that already exists but that the student makes unique in some way.

    Suggest that the students consider which name or part of their name (first, middle, or last name) they would use as the eponym.

3. Move the students into small groups to share their answers.

Variations

Use a television talk show format to interview students on how their names came to be associated with the particular thing they chose.

The students could also put together a newsletter in which they could report on the many contributions of the class as reflected in the number of things named after them.

This could be made into a craft project where students draw or create the item to which their name would be connected.

---

*The eponyms used in this activity were suggested by the article "The Word as Person" by Don Farrant, in *Sky Magazine,* Halsey Publishing Company, 1992.

Eponym Worksheet

Connect the names in column 1 with the item in column 2 associated with each person.

Column 1   *Column 2*

1. Nellie Melba
   Australian soprano

   a. railroad car with sleeping quarters

2. James T. Brundell
   Seven Earl of Cardigan
   British General

   b. loose woman's trouser gathered at the knee

3. Amelia Bloomer
   American feminist

   c. thin slices of crisp toast

4. George M. Pullman
   American industrialist

   d. alphabetical characters represented by raised dots used by sightless people

5. Jeanne Antoinette Poisson
   Marquise de Pompadour

   e. collarless jacket opened down the front

6. Louis Braille
   Frenchman

   f. the style of dressing one's hair high over the forehead

7. Robert W. Bunsen
   German professor

   g. refusal do do business with a person or company in order to bring about a settlement

8. Captain Charles Boycott
   Irish land agent

   h. a horse race such as the one in Kentucky

9. Edward Smith Stanley
   Twelfth Earl of Derby

   i. a unit of electrical power

10. James Watt
    Scottish engineer

    j. type of gas burner

Bonus Questions

11. What did Samuel F. B. Morse invent? _____

12. Can you think of any other eponymous words? _____

_____

_____

With what would you like to have your own name associated?

- a type of food

- an article of clothing

- a game or sport

- a new invention

Chapter 1—Suggested Student Readings

Anderson, Eloise A. *Carlos Goes to School.* New York: Warner, 1973.

Ayer, Jacqueline. *NuDang and His Kite.* New York: Harcourt Brace, 1959.

Bales, Carol Ann. *Kevin Cloud: Chippewa Boy in the City.* Chicago: Reilly & Lee, 1972.

Batdorf, Carol. *Tinka: A Day in a Little Girl's Life.* Blaine, WA: Hancock House, 1990.

Demi. *Liang and the Magic Paintbrush.* New York: Harper & Row, 1982.

Hamilton, Virginia. *Drylongso.* New York: Harcourt Brace Jovanovich, 1993.

Head, Barry, & Jim Sequin. *Who Am I?* Illinois: Hubbard, 1975.

Hoffman, Mary, & Caroline Binch. *Amazing Grace.* New York: Dial, 1991.

Saiki, Patsy Sumie. *Sachie, a Daughter of Hawaii.* Honolulu, HI: Kisaku, 1977.

San Souci, Robert. *The Legend of Scarface.* New York: Doubleday, 1978.

Wolf, Janet. *Adelaide to Zeke.* New York: Harper & Row, 1977.

Eponym Worksheet Answers

1.	c	6.	d
2.	e	7.	j
3.	b	8.	g
4.	a	9.	h
5.	f	10.	i

Chapter 2

Pride and Joy

Celebrating Self

*There is a vitality, a life-force, an energy, a quickening
that is translated through you into action and because
there is only one of you in all of time, this expression is
unique. And if you block it, it will never exist through
any other medium and be lost.*
—Martha Graham

Introduction

*To finally recognize our own invisibility,
is to finally be on the path toward visibility.*
—Mitsuye Yamada

*Cassie Louise Lightfoot can fly. That's right. Even though she is only eight
years old and in the third grade, she can fly. This means she is free to go
wherever she wants.*

*It's easy, she says. "All you need is somewhere to go you can't get to any
other way."*

*Cassie begins her adventure while sleeping in Tar Beach, the rooftop of the
building where she lives in Harlem.*

*"Lying on the roof in the night, with stars and skyscraper buildings all
around me, made me feel rich, like I owned all that I could see."*

*All she sees—the bridge, the union building and, of course, the ice cream
factory—Cassie claims for herself and her family.*

The next time she goes flying she will have to take her brother, Be Be, with her otherwise he'll tell on her.*

Chapter 2 is about celebrating yourself, taking pride in who you are and enjoying being yourself. Students learn that they can love themselves even when there are things they don't like about themselves. Like Cassie, they are invited to fly to a magical place where they meet an extraordinary person and receive a special gift—themselves.

9 Favorite Things

We can only be said to be alive in those moments when our hearts are conscious of our treasures.
—Thornton Wilder

Purpose

This activity works well as an ice breaker. It allows students to get to know each other better through sharing about things that they like.

Procedure

1. Hand out copies of the Favorite Things Worksheet.

2. Have students walk around the room interviewing each other by asking their fellow students one of the questions on the worksheet.

3. In each box on the worksheet, the student is to write the name of the student interviewed and his or her answer to the question. Each of the nine boxes is to be filled in with the name and answer of a different student.

4. Let the students know that they will have about ten minutes to complete the activity. Call time when you see that most of the students are finished.

5. Bring the students together in a circle. Focusing on one student at a time, ask the rest of the group what they learned about this student.

*Tar Beach by Faith Ringgold (New York: Crown, 1991).

Continue around the class until each student's favorite things have been revealed.

Variation

If you want to reduce the amount of time required to do this activity, you can divide the class into three teams of approximately ten students each and have them interview just the classmates on their team. They can do the sharing in their teams as well.

Favorite Things Worksheet

1. Name ——————— Favorite Color ———————	2. Name ——————— Favorite Food ———————	3. Name ——————— Favorite Music ———————
4. Name ——————— Favorite Book ———————	5. Name ——————— Favorite Subject in School ———————	6. Name ——————— Favorite Hobby ———————
7. Name ——————— Favorite TV Program ———————	8. Name ——————— Favorite Family Activity ———————	9. Name ——————— Favorite Thing to Do with Friends ———————

The students can brainstorm other topics and create their own worksheet.

10   If You Were . . .

*If one is lucky, a solitary fantasy
can totally transform one million realities.*

—Maya Angelou

Purpose

This activity serves as a good warm-up exercise and energizer. It helps students get to know their fellow classmates at a safe, low level of self-disclosure.

Student answers can be studied for patterns that relate to their self-identity by looking to see if there are common characteristics among the chosen items.

Procedure

1. Hand out copies of the If You Were . . . Worksheet.

2. Have students mill around the room interviewing each other. For example, "If you were an animal, what animal would you be? What characteristic of that animal do you like?"

3. Each box on the worksheet is to be filled out about a different student, so that nine classmates are interviewed during the process.

4. Inform the class that they have about ten minutes to do the activity.

5. When the students are finished, bring them together in a circle and have them share what they discovered about each other.

If You Were . . . Worksheet

1. Name _____

Animal

_____

Characteristic

_____

2. Name _____

Color

_____

Characteristic

_____

3. Name _____

Song

_____

Characteristic

_____

4. Name _____

Musical Instrument

_____

Characteristic

_____

5. Name _____

Room in a House

_____

Characteristic

_____

6. Name _____

Type of Food

_____

Characteristic

_____

7. Name _____

Car

_____

Characteristic

_____

8. Name _____

Famous Person

_____

Characteristic

_____

9. Name _____

Folktale Character

_____

Characteristic

_____

The students can brainstorm other topics and create their own worksheet.

11   I Just Wrote to Say, "I Love You"

*We all feel more beautiful when we are loved.
And when you have self-love you are always beautiful.*
—Alice Walker

Purpose

To support students in remembering to love themselves even when it may be hard to do so.

Materials

an envelope for each student
a piece of paper (preferably lined) or stationery for each student
pens or pencils

Procedure

1. Ask students to think of a time when they felt really sad—when they were angry, depressed, disappointed, jealous, embarrassed, or all of these at once.

2. Then, brainstorm with your students ways in which they were able to snap out of these negative feelings—they listened to music, someone told them a joke, they got a hug, they read an enjoyable book, and so forth.

3. Now ask them to imagine some time in the future when they might get into that frame of mind again: when they might think they are feeling so sad they'll never be happy again; when they might start believing they are really rotten and useless; when they are in such trouble they can't see any way out; when they wish the earth would just open up and swallow them!

4. Ask the students to consider what they would need to hear to snap out of the negative frame of mind. What reminders, examples, sayings, stories, and so on would put them back in touch with the fact that they are lovable and capable persons?

5. Once they know what they would need to hear, tell them to write themselves each a personal letter—to be opened and read only when they need it.

6. You might suggest that in their letter they remind themselves that they knew there was a possibility they would feel this way some time—and that there is another way of feeling. Ask them to write whatever they know will soothe them, humor them, and get them back in touch with loving themselves.

7. When they have finished their letters, have your students put them in the envelopes, seal them, and mark them TOP SECRET. Recommend that they put them in a special place and save them until needed.

12 "I Love Myself Even When . . ."

*F*riendship with oneself is all-important, because without it one cannot be friends with anyone else in the world.

—Eleanor Roosevelt

Purpose

This activity lets students experience loving themselves unconditionally by distinguishing between (1) who they *are* and (2) what they *do* or *have*. In this activity, they acknowledge themselves for all the things they like about themselves. Then they consider what they don't like and find ways to accept themselves anyway.

Materials

art paper (12″ × 18″)
colored markers or crayons
paste or glue

Procedure

1. Have each student bring a recent photograph of him- or herself to class.

2. Read the story *Mama, Do You Love Me?* by Barbara M. Joose (San Francisco: Chronicle Books, 1991).

3. Give each student a piece of art paper and ask him or her to glue the picture in the center of the paper.

4. Now provide the following instructions:

> "Next to your picture, with a colored marking pen or crayon—pick a color that you like—write or draw one thing about yourself that you like, appreciate, or are proud of. Consider different aspects of yourself—your appearance, your talents, your personality, and so on."

> "Now turn the paper over. Using a marker of a color you don't like, write or draw one thing you dislike about yourself."

> "Turn back to the front side. Write (or draw) another thing you like about yourself. (Use a color you like.) Then turn the paper over and write a second thing you dislike about yourself. (Use a color you don't like.)"

> "Continue to write (or draw) things you like about yourself on the picture side and things you dislike about yourself on the opposite side, using the appropriate colored marking pens for each item." (To keep this simpler for younger children, limit it to one or two things they like/dislike, and give them the frame sentence: "I love myself when . . .")

> "After you have written all the negative things about yourself you can think of, read each criticism and then write above it the words, 'I love myself even when . . .' "

> "You are acknowledging that you are lovable with or without your faults; the faults are related to what you *have* or what you *do*, not who you *are*. You, the person, are completely worthy of being loved."

5. Have students get into a group. Ask them to take turns showing their pictures to the group and explaining the things they like and don't like about themselves.

6. When everyone in each group has finished, you may have them hang their pictures, with the positive side showing, on the bulletin board. Otherwise, instruct them to take the pictures home and hang them up.

Note: This activity invites a higher degree of self-disclosure than the earlier ones. Let students know that it is up to them how much personal information they want to share during this and all future activities. They are in control of their answers, and they are always free to pass.

13 To Change the Things I Can

*Growth itself
contains the germ
of happiness.*
—Pearl Buck

Purpose

In the previous activity, "I Love Myself Even When . . . ," students identified some things they like about themselves and some things they don't like. This exercise, geared for older students, helps them realize that although there may be some personal traits we cannot change, other characteristics are within our power to control and improve.

Procedure

1. Have students refer to their drawings done for the earlier activity "I Love Myself Even When . . . ," using the side of things they don't like about themselves as a starting point.

2. Hand out copies of the To Change the Things I Can Worksheet.

3. Now, give the students the following instructions:

   "Looking at the back of your drawing where you wrote or drew pictures of things you don't like about yourself, pick those aspects of yourself that you feel you can change and write them in column 1 of your worksheet."

   "Any aspects of yourself that you feel you cannot change, please put down in column 2."

   "If you are not sure whether you can change a particular characteristic, put it in column 3."

   "Are there any questions? Anyone who is unclear or doesn't understand the instructions?"

4. After the students have had time to fill out the top part of their worksheet, have them get together with a partner, in small groups, or as a full class to discuss the process so far.

5. Next, conduct a full-class discussion on how people can change things they don't like about themselves.

Using your own worksheet as an example and/or asking a couple of students to volunteer their answers, pick a trait that can be changed and have your students brainstorm ways of producing the desired change. Here is an example:

Something I want to change
—Shyness

Things I can do
—Tell myself I'm O.K.
—Practice talking more when I'm with friends.
—Force myself to raise my hand more often in class.
—Really do my homework so I feel confident about what I have to say.
—Talk with people who are more outgoing and ask them for advice.

6. Ask students to fill in the bottom of their worksheets.

   "Pick one area that you want to work on changing. List some things you can do this week to start to make the change."

7. Have students return to their partner, small group, or full group to share their action plans. If they need help thinking of more things they can do this week, let them ask for ideas from their classmates.

8. Set aside time later in the week to have students share their progress in making the changes they identified.

To Change The Things I Can Worksheet

*Things I Can
Change*

*Things I Cannot
Change*

*Things I'm Not
Sure About*

_____   _____   _____

_____   _____   _____

_____   _____   _____

_____   _____   _____

_____   _____   _____

_____   _____   _____

Something I want to change: _____

Things I will do this week:

_____

_____

_____

_____

14 Your Special Gift

I believe I'm here for a reason. And I think a little bit of the reason is to throw little torches out to lead people through the dark. When you're kind to someone in trouble, you hope they'll remember and be kind to someone else. And it'll become like a wildfire. Each person helping someone who then helps someone else, and so on. And I'm afraid that I'm going to wake up one day, and the wind will be so strong that no torch can bear up to it. I think that's my biggest fear. That I won't be strong enough to keep throwing the torches. But I know I'll keep trying.

—Whoopi Goldberg

Background

This activity introduces students to the idea of a special guide. As much as anything, it is meant to connect them with their own inner wisdom.

Special guides appear in literature from many cultures. One example is the Biblical Story of Joseph and his brothers, which also appears as an African folk-tale. In Hawaii the same tale is known as "Aükele and the Water of Life," and related tales are found among the Maori of New Zealand as well as in Tonga, the Marquesas, and Samoa. Familiar themes are encountered in cultures ranging from Zulu to Eskimo to Semitic.

A version entitled "The Kindly Ghost" is including in *World Tales*, collected by Idries Shah (New York: Harcourt Brace Jovanovich, 1979).

You may want to read this or another story about a spirit guide, fairy godmother, or genie to stimulate the children's imagination before doing this activity.

Purpose

The purpose of this activity is to get students to realize that each of them is a unique individual and that, although we all have a lot in common, no two of us are exactly the same. We each have our own personalities, our own combinations of traits and talents—and we each have special contributions to make to our families, friends, and society. It may be done in conjunction with Activity 7, "Brand Names," since both activities emphasize each student being special.

Materials

drawing paper, one piece per student
drawing supplies, such as crayons or colored markers

Procedure

1. Introduce the activity to your students by letting them know that they will be doing an imagination exercise. In the process they will receive an object that in some way symbolizes one of their qualities or characteristics.

2. Discuss with your class how an object can symbolize a quality (a heart meaning love, a sword for commitment, a diamond for purity, a lotus blossom for beauty, a bear for courage, a picture of a saint for goodness, a jester for humor, a wand for creativity, a musical instrument for harmony, and so on).

3. Draw a few common symbols on the board and ask your students to brainstorm what these represent. Ask students to suggest objects that symbolize or represent joy, compassion, courage, peace, and so forth.

4. Have the students sit in a comfortable position and close their eyes. Tell them to relax by taking a few deep breaths. Ask them to imagine the following (give the instructions slowly, pausing after each line to give the students enough time to create an image in their minds):

   Imagine you are opening a door that leads outside, and walk out.

   You notice that you are stepping out onto a large field of grass.

   As you look around, you notice the brightness of the light, the vividness of the colors; the grass; the sky; the sun.

   You can feel the light breeze blowing gently across your face.

   And you can smell the grass and the scent of the flowers.

   Now you realize you are about to go on a special journey—a really fun adventure.

   To get where you are going, you will need a special means of transportation.

   As you look up, you see this wonderful, amazing, magical, flying carpet, which seems to appear out of nowhere and sort of dances around in the sky before swooping down beside you.

   As you see the magic carpet landing next to you—hovering just above the ground so you can get on it easily—you step onto the carpet and sit down on it.

As it takes off again, you feel it lift up. You literally feel yourself rising above the ground as the carpet takes you higher and higher. You may even feel the air growing cooler as you rise higher above the earth.

You find you feel safe —knowing you can't fall off or be hurt.

As you look around, you can see how small everything now looks on the ground.

As you continue to fly higher and higher on your magic carpet, you begin to approach a very large mountain, and because you are flying so high, you approach the mountain at one of its highest peaks.

Now you notice that the magic carpet takes you to a place on the mountain where it can land.

You realize that this place is very special -- almost like a large cave. The walls are encrusted with jewel-like crystals, which glisten in the light.

Somehow you become aware that this is the home of a very special guide.

As you begin to feel this person's presence, your guide appears, holding a small golden chest with a special gift inside just for you.

As you are handed the chest, you are first taken with how beautiful it is. Before opening it, you are told that the gift inside represents the gift you are to the world.

As you begin to open the chest, you can see the gift. As you take it out of the chest, you hold it and touch it. As you explore what it feels like with your hands and look at it from all sides, you let the connection between this object and the special gift that you are become clearer and clearer.

Then your guide tells you to feel free to ask any questions you have about this gift or to say anything you want to at this time. (Long pause—one minute.)

As you now begin to realize that it is time to leave, you thank your guide for this special gift. Knowing you can always visit with this person any time you want, you can say good-bye for now.

And now you put your gift back into the chest and bring it with you.

As you walk to the entrance of the cave, you get back on the magic carpet.

As you feel it lift you away—out of the cave, and around the mountain; out into the open air; and back toward the earth—you contemplate this special gift. Soon you find yourself coming back toward the field of grass where the carpet picked you up; and as you approach the field, you find yourself landing gently.

As you step off the magic carpet, you bring your gift with you.

You watch the magic carpet fly away, and now you make your journey through time and space, and return to the present moment in this room.

5. Ask the students to take their time, and when they are ready, to open their eyes. Instruct them to let the other students come back on their own, and to just wait quietly until everyone is ready. (If some students are slow to return, you may want to touch them gently on their shoulders and help them become reoriented.)

6. When all the students have opened their eyes, ask them to take a few deep breaths and stretch their arms and legs.

7. Have the students do a drawing of the gift given to them by their guide, using crayons and a piece of white paper.

8. As with any guided fantasy or imagination process, there is no right or wrong way of doing it. Whatever the students experienced is fine. If students say that they do not remember the gift, invite them to draw what the gift would be if they *did* remember, or simply to make it up.

9. Divide the class into small groups (perhaps their support teams; see Activity 30) to have them share their drawings and other aspects of the experience. You may want to post the drawings on a bulletin board or tell students to hang them up somewhere at home.

15 Highlights of My Life

*When I was born, I was so surprised
I couldn't talk for a year and a half.*

—Gracie Allen

Purpose

One's life experiences make up a significant part of one's identity. The aim of this activity is for students to reflect on the major events of their lives and consider how these events contributed to making them unique.

Materials

Drawing supplies, such as pencils, crayons, or colored markers

Procedure

1. Hand out copies of the Highlights of My Life—I Worksheet.

2. Have students draw a picture in each frame representing a highlight event in their lives. Ask them to recall moments when they felt special or felt especially happy or successful.

3. Students can then get into groups of six or eight and take turns sharing their highlights.

Highlights of My Life—I Worksheet

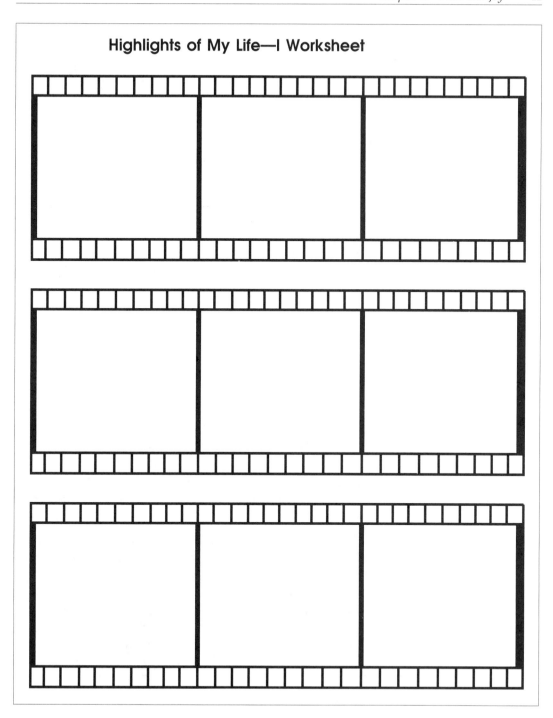

16 Award Winners

Silent gratitude isn't very much use to anyone.
—G. B. Stern

Purpose

Most students are probably aware of the numerous awards shows on television, such as the Oscars, the Grammies, and the MTV awards. This activity provides an opportunity for students to acknowledge the positive qualities they recognize in their classmates. It completes the sequence of activities on names by having each award named for the student who receives it. You can also record this activity and play it at a parent meeting or school assembly.

Note: Please read the next activity, "Play TV," before doing this one in case you want to integrate the two.

Procedure

1. Divide the class into small groups.

2. Give each group the names of a few other students in the class to acknowledge at the awards ceremony. (Each student receives one award.)

3. Ask the students, when they get the names, not to let anyone know whose acknowledgments they are going to do. The surprise factor will make it more fun.

4. Instruct each group to take the names one at a time. Tell them to consider the things about the person that they like, admire, and appreciate—those things that make the person special.

5. Now that they have a list of qualities and contributions for which to acknowledge the person, direct each group of students to think of a way of summarizing, in the form of a special award, what that person has done for the group. For example, there might be a person who gets the *thoughtfulness award* for always being kind to people, helping people who are having problems, and so on. Or there might be a good *humor award* for a person who lightens up heavy situations and is always good for a laugh.

6. Hand out copies of the Awards Worksheet and have the students complete one certificate for each of the names they received. The award is named after the student who will receive it, and the person's special attribute is filled in on the line provided. Encourage students to decorate each certificate with colors and designs that make it personal to the recipient.

7. When all the groups are finished, they are to bring their awards to the awards ceremony (class circle). You, as master of ceremonies, will call on each group to make their awards. To add to the fun, they can pretend they are Oscar presenters and call for "the envelope, please." Be sure that each group does a good job of explaining and displaying the award and letting the winner feel the full sincerity of their acknowledgment.

   You may want to discuss how to receive compliments graciously.

8. Close with a discussion using questions such as:

   "What award did you receive at the awards ceremony?"

   "How did it feel to receive this compliment?"

   "Do you ever acknowledge yourself for these good qualities? If you don't, take the time to do that now."

Follow-up Activity

Students can list people in their lives who deserve to be acknowledged for the things they have done for the students in the past month. The students could then be encouraged to make awards for these people or, in some other creative way, acknowledge these people for their contributions.

Awards Worksheet

AWARD
is presented to

for

Awards Worksheet Sample

MALIKAH

AWARD
is presented to

Malikah Brown

for

Being a Special Friend

17 Play TV

*We can't take any credit for our talents.
It's how we use them that counts.*

—Madeleine L'Engle

Background

The culture of television and video probably has more influence on our children than any other aspect of their environment, what with video games, video tapes, television (including MTV and other cable channels), and so forth.

This activity is one of a series scattered throughout the book that uses video-recording equipment to engage students in ways that are highly motivating, great fun, and very powerful.

Materials

> video recorder (camcorder)
> VCR
> TV monitor
> blank video tape

Many schools have video equipment available for classroom use. Otherwise you should be able to borrow equipment from a colleague or parent, have equipment donated by a local business group, or rent it from a video store.

Depending on the age of your students, you can have them run the equipment, involve older students or parents, or do it yourself.

Anecdotal Material

Although some students may be camera shy and may need some coaching to participate, in my experience most children are excited by this opportunity to "show their stuff."

In one group of visually impaired students with whom I conducted a three-day Self-Esteem and Responsibility Workshop, the use of videotaping proved to be transformative, especially for one child.

The setup was a talent show along the lines of "The Tonight Show." One student reveled in his role of announcer, even ad libbing commercials. Another student was the host, while others told jokes, sang, or demonstrated some other talent.

One student in the program was a twenty-year-old who looked, dressed, and acted like a child of ten. Twe was a Vietnamese girl who had lost her parents during the Vietnam War and then had lost her sight as bombs exploded near her while she was escaping her homeland.

Now blind, she found herself living in a foreign country with a different language and customs. To get attention, she acted fearful, timid, shy, and clinging. She had a tendency to whine, complain, and relate to life as a victim—understandable, given her life experiences.

After much coaxing, however, Twe reluctantly agreed to take part in the talent show. As she sang a song in her native Vietnamese, the change in her demeanor was profound. She became confident, strong, proud, and powerful.

Even though none of us understood the lyrics and the sound of the language was unfamiliar, we were all moved to tears by the poignancy of the moment. By reconnecting with her cultural roots, Twe felt at home with herself for the first time in quite awhile.

By the way, Twe is now living on her own and feeling quite liberated by her ability to be independent.

Purpose

This activity will introduce students to the idea of using video recording as a learning tool.

It will also serve as a means of helping students integrate the material presented so far in this course.

In developing this project, seek to balance the need for structure, so that students don't feel lost or overwhelmed, with the need for meaningful involvement that is necessary for the students to feel ownership for the results, commitment to doing well, and pride in their success.

Procedure

1. To support students in being comfortable with using video equipment in the classroom, initiate a discussion along the following lines:

   "How many of you have video recorders or camcorders at home?"

   "How many of you have seen yourself on TV (that is, on video playback equipment)?"

   "How did you feel about seeing yourself?"

   "What did you like about seeing yourself on TV?"

   "Was there anything that you didn't like?"

"How many of you have run the equipment yourself—both the camcorder and the VCR?"

2. Continue by saying:

"In this class we are going to produce our own TV show. We are going to do this as a way of helping us remember what we are learning, perhaps using it to teach others and because it will be fun."

3a. *Structured Approach:* Use the previous activity, "Award Winners," as a way of structuring the video activity.

3b. *Creative Approach:* Say to students:

"Let's start with brainstorming different kinds of TV programs, and then we can pick which type to use after we talk about possible topics for the show."

"So what are the various types of TV shows you watch?"

Invite student responses such as:

- situation comedies
- news
- dramatic shows
- cartoons
- talk shows
- home video shows
- musical variety shows
- music videos
- advertisements
- award shows

4. Next hand out the Part I—Key Learnings and have the students discuss what they remember about these topics. Then have the students vote on which topic would work best for making a TV program. A simple method is to have each student vote for one topic and use the one that gets the most votes.

5. Once the topic of the show has been selected, refer back to the brainstormed list of types of programs and discuss with your students the advantages and disadvantages of each type as it relates to the topic that was selected.

6. Consider how long the program will be, what will actually happen, in what sequence, and how long each sequence will be. Encourage students to identify how they would like to contribute and what part they would like to play—director, camera person, lighting technician, musician, costumer, writer, actor, comedian, announcer, and so forth.

7. Give students time to prepare.

8. Videotape a dress rehearsal, and invite students to give each other positive feedback as to what worked and what could be improved.

9. Videotape the final show and play it back for students' enjoyment.

10. Discuss with students who else they would like to have see the video and what they learned in the process.

Part I—Key Learnings

I am somebody special.

It is okay for me to say, "I love myself." This is not bragging. It is knowing that I am worthwhile.

My being here is important.

I love myself even when I do things that I do not like.

I belong here.

I was born for a good reason.

I am unique.

I was born with special gifts and talents and it is my responsibility to do something with these.

I have something of value to share.

Note: At the end of each of the four parts of this book, a Teacher Checklist is provided. Please take a minute to reflect on the extent to which you have integrated the lessons of these two chapters.

Part I—Teacher Checklist:
Being Aware of Personal Biases
and Low Self-Esteem Indicators

❑ Do I think that teaching is an important profession?

❑ Do I have confidence in my ability to find ways of being successful with all students?

❑ Am I able to love myself even when I do things that are not successful?

❑ Are my relationships healthy and do I feel capable of loving and being loved?

❑ Do I feel powerful in being able to direct my life toward my goals?

❑ Have I ever been at the receiving end of some form of discrimination, and have I been able to make peace with these incidents?

❑ Am I open-minded enough to accept other points of view as being equally valid?

❑ Do I pay attention and give positive feedback to all students equally?

❑ Am I willing to pay closer attention to my interaction with students; noticing which ones I am more or less comfortable with, which ones I expect the most from, which ones I call on the most, praise and encourage the most, and so forth?

❑ If I discover cultural, ethnic, or gender biases, am I willing to correct these?

Chapter 2—Suggested Student Readings

Adoff, Arnold. *Black Is Brown Is Tan.* New York: Harper & Row, 1973.

Dr. Seuss. *My Book about Me.* New York: Random House, 1969.

Ets, Maria Hall. *Bad Boy, Good Boy.* New York: Crowell, 1967.

Greenfield, Eloise. *Daydreamers.* New York: Dial, 1981.

Joosse, Barbara M. & Barbara Lavallee. *Mama, Do You Love Me?* San Francisco: Chronicle Books, 1991.

Lee, Jeanne M. *Ba-Nam.* New York: Henry Holt, 1987.

Nixon, Joan L. *The Gift.* New York: Macmillan, 1983.

Paek, M. *Aekyung's Dream.* Chicago: Children's Press, 1978.

Pittman, Helena. *The Gift of the Willows.* Minneapolis, MN: Carolrhoda, 1988.

Politi, Leo. *The Nicest Gift.* New York: Scribner's, 1973.

Ringgold, Faith. *Tar Beach.* New York: Crown, 1991.

Seed, Jenny. *Ntombi's Song.* Boston: Beacon Press, 1987.

Shah, Idries. *World Tales.* New York: Harcourt Brace Jovanovich, 1979.

Uchida, Yoshiko. *Makoto, the Smallest Boy.* New York: Thomas Y. Crowell, 1970.

Walker, Alice, & Catherine Deeter. *Finding the Green Stone.* New York: Harcourt Brace Jovanovich, 1991.

Self-Esteem and Interdependence

Freedom to Be We

*N*obody, but nobody can make it here alone.
—Maya Angelou

	Experience (Internal)	Express (External)
Others	Interdependence	Social Responsibility
Self	Independence	Personal Responsibility

Chapter *3*

Cultural Identity
Roots from Which to Grow

To be rooted is perhaps the most important and least recognized need of the human soul.
—Simone Weil

Introduction

What families have in common the world around is that they are the place where people learn who they are and how to be that way.
—Jean Illsey Clarke

Once upon a time, long ago, lived a young girl named Tokoyo. Her father, who was a samurai, taught Tokoyo how to ride a horse and how to shoot a bow and arrow. He also taught her the virtues of courage and discipline as well as the warrior's duty to protect the weak.

All of these skills were to come in handy, as Tokoyo would soon find out.

One day, it happened that Japan's ruler—apparently under some type of spell that caused him to fear even his most devoted knights—banished Tokoyo's father into exile.

After weeks of grieving for the loss of her father, Tokoyo decided to join him. She made this difficult journey alone—across mountains, hiding from bandits—until she reached the sea that she would have to boat across to get to the island where her father was.

She survived her encounter with the ghost ship that haunted the waters.

When she next heard the sobbing of a young girl who was to be the human sacrifice demanded by the demon sea serpent, Tokoyo felt duty-bound as a samurai to help her by taking her place.

Not only did she kill the evil sea serpent, but she also discovered the secret to breaking the spell that had caused the ruler's madness.

Reunited, and blessed by the ruler with many honors for her courage and loyalty, Tokoyo and her father lived in peace and prosperity for the rest of their lives.*

Welcome!

You, your family, your ancestors, and your cultural heritage belong here. That is the message of this chapter. Families—no matter what size or shape—are the basic units of love and support for children. The ratio of nuclear families in all U.S. households dropped from 40 percent in 1970 to 26 percent in 1990, according to the U.S. Census Bureau. This means that three out of four children in today's schools come from a home with a family configuration other than Mom, Dad, and kids all living under the same roof. Schools must reach out to families and get them involved in their youngsters' education. In order for this to happen, members of the family need to feel welcome and wanted.

The activities in this chapter invite students to learn about their ancestors and share about their families so that they feel that their life experiences are legitimate and that they indeed belong in this classroom. A sense of belonging, a feeling of being connected with the group, is an essential ingredient of healthy self-esteem. This is among the best arguments for a multicultural approach to education.

By virtue of what is and is not included in the curriculum, schools play a crucial role in establishing what knowledge, values, and life experiences are deemed worthwhile. Students whose culture is reflected in their school will feel validated; their "cultural capital"† will be increased.

Conversely, ethnic groups who are not included will feel devalued and their cultural capital will be depleted. Students in this situation face the dilemma of either rejecting their own culture and embracing that of the school in order to succeed, or negating the value of school in order to protect their self-pride. This is a choice no one should have to make.

Similar to the theory of cultural capital is the "poker chip" analogy of self-esteem. The idea is that students who have a history of success and positive acknowledgment possess a sizable stack of chips—a psychological

---

*The Samurai's Daughter by Robert D. San Souci, pictures by Stephen T. Johnson (New York: Dial, 1992).

†For further discussion of the idea of "cultural capital," see Pierre Bourdien, "The Forms of Capital," in *Handbook of Theory and Research for the Sociology of Education,* ed. John G. Richardson (New York: Greenwood Press, 1986).

bank account of self-valuing experiences, if you will—from which to draw in dealing with life's challenges. If they take a risk and don't succeed, the one or two chips they lose are not significant,given the total number they possess. They are able to stay in the game.

On the other hand, students who have had few opportunities to experience success and receive positive recognition have a great deal to lose, given that one or two chips may be all they have with which to play. Dropping out of the game may seem the only logical thing to do.

Schools have a responsibility to empower students by giving them a chance to build up their self-esteem "chips" and to increase their cultural capital.

18 Willkommen, Bienvenue, Welcome

Background

Language plays a critical role in our cultural identity. It is how we express ourselves. Beyond words, language communicates a certain style or personality. Language embodies a people's history and geography. It has texture and color, rhythm and tempo. Language can convey a shared perspective toward life and a sense of humor. Many of these elements can get lost in translation.

Much has been written about bilingual education. Controversy revolves around whether or not it is effective and whether or not lack of proficiency in English is the major reason for the academic failure of language-minority students.

The purpose of bilingual education is also debated. Is the objective for students to learn English as quickly as possible because this is the key to equal opportunity? Is the point to teach academic subjects in the students' primary language so that they do not fall behind in subject matter content while they are learning English? Should the vision be true bilingualism and biliteracy—a nation of people who are linguistically competent and thus better able to function in a world of many languages and cultures?

However these debates are resolved, the fact remains that building a child's self-esteem in today's multicultural classroom must include a sensitivity to each student's linguistic heritage.

Students should be encouraged to use their primary language around school:

- As part of the learning process (for example, in cooperative learning groups made up of students from the same ethnic group on at least some occasions)

- in elective subjects and extracurricular activities

- in writing for school newspapers and other official school communications

- during assemblies, award presentations and other schoolwide functions.

The following activity is one step in this direction.

Purpose

The purpose of this activity is to create a welcoming classroom for all students, especially those for whom English is not their primary language.

Procedure

1. Determine the native languages of the students in your class, and learn how to say "Welcome" in each language. You may want to include other languages that your students will find in their community or will be studying later in school. You also may want to ask your students what other languages interest them.

    In addition to the word "Welcome," you might also want to teach the children a few other words or phrases in each language, such as "Thank you."

2. Prepare a large banner to hang in front of the room with the word "Welcome" on it. Each day, use a different language.

3. Have the students practice saying the word during the morning class meeting or "My Circle of Friends" time (Activity 28). When one student has finished sharing, he or she passes the turn to the next student in the circle by saying "Welcome" and that student's name.

4. If visitors come into your classroom during this time, have the students greet them by saying "Welcome" in the language of the day.

5. Use other simple words from the focus language throughout the day whenever possible.

6. You may want to read with your students the book *Welcome Roberto! Bienvenido, Roberto!* by Mary Senfozo (Chicago: Follett, 1969).

English	Welcome	Thank you
German	Willkommen	Danke schön
French	Bienvenu	Merci
Italian	Benvenuti	Grazie
Spanish	Bienvenido	Gracias
Portuguese	Boas-vindas	Obrigado
Japanese	Inashai mase	Arigato
Chinese	Huan yin	Xie-xie
Vietnamese	Chao mung	Cám on

19 Family Values

In Vietnam traditional values have deep roots. When the heavy winds blow reeds bend, but when the winds cease, they once again stand straight and tall.
—Vuong G. Thuy

Purpose

Many children today live in what would be considered nontraditional family structures—divorced parents, single parents, blended families, same-gender parents, and so forth. The purpose of this activity is for students to feel proud of their families, whatever their situation.

Materials

colored paper cut in the shape of leaves
art paper
pens
glue

Procedure

1. Read to the students *All Kinds of Families* by Norman Simon (Niles, IL: Whitman Albut, 1976).

2. Write the word *family* on the board and ask your students to help define the term. Consider questions such as:

"What is a family?"

"What makes someone a member of a family?"

"When you think of your family, whom do you include?"

"Are there people whom you don't see very often who are still part of your family?"

"Are there people who feel like family but really are not?"

"What are some things that families do together?"

3. Now, write the word *values* on the board and ask your students' help to define this term.

Consider question such as:

"What does the word *values* mean?"

"If by *values* we mean the most important qualities of someone or something, then what do you value most about your family?"

"If by *values* we mean our most cherished beliefs or principles, what values did George Washington stand for? How about Mahatma Gandhi, Chief Seattle, Martin Luther King, Mother Teresa, Nelson Mandela, Cesar Chavez, Emperor Hirohito, Shirley Chisholm?"

4. Distribute the art supplies. You may want to have the students work in teams so that they can share some of the materials.

5. Discuss the idea of a family tree, which is used to diagram the lineage of a family, and say that we are going to create our own family tree in a somewhat different way.

Rather than tracing the branches from parent to parent, generation by generation, we are going to display our existing family in the broadest possible terms.

We are also going to identify which values each of our family members represent to us, values such as:

love	honesty	hardworkingness
caring	truth	fun
support	integrity	spirituality
understanding	beauty	strength
listening	elegance	success
appreciating	creativity	loyalty
sensitivity	intelligence	organization

6. Instruct the students to start with themselves:

"Take a leaf, write your name on it and write one value that you stand for. Paste your leaf somewhere near the center of the page.

"Next, think of the family members to whom you feel closest. Write their names on separate leaves, and also write down the value that each person represents for you. Glue these leaves on the page near yours.

"Continue the activity until you have done a leaf for everyone you consider part of your family."

7. When the students are finished, have them share their family trees with each other in small groups or as a full class. You may want to post the finished work on a bulletin board, or invite the students to bring them home to share.

20 Highlights of My Ancestors

*We all grow up with the weight of history on us.
Our ancestors dwell in the attics of our brains
as they do in the spiraling chains of knowledge
hidden in every cell of our bodies.*

—Shirley Abbott

Purpose

This activity is intended to inspire students to develop pride in their family history and cultural background.

Materials

drawing supplies, such as pencils, crayons, or colored markers

Procedure

1. Students will probably need to do some research before beginning this activity. As a homework assignment, give each student a copy of the Highlights of My Ancestors Worksheet—I and ask them to complete it at home by asking questions of their parents or guardians, grandparents, and other family members.

2. In class, hand out copies of Highlights of My Ancestors Worksheet—II and ask students to draw a picture of a "highlight" event from their family's history in each of the boxes.

Each row of picture frames can represent a generation of events:

Row 1—parents' generation
Row 2—grandparents' generation
Row 3—previous generations

3. When the students are finished with their drawings, have them share in small groups or as a full class.

Highlights of My Ancestors Worksheet—I

Parents' Generation

In what country were your parents or guardians born?

Was there anything special or unusual about the circumstances of their birth?

What do they remember most about their childhood?

What happened to them as adults that was a highlight?

What major events have most effected their lives (moving to another country or another part of the country, getting married, having children, buying their first home, the death of someone dear, etc.)?

Grandparents' Generation

In what country were your grandparents born?

Was there anything special or unusual about the circumstances of their birth?

What do they remember most about their childhood?

What happened to them as adults that was a highlight?

What major events have most effected their lives (moving to another country or another part of the country, getting married, having children, buying their first home, the death of someone dear, etc.)?

Previous Generations

What can you find out about the parents of your grandparents and any of your ancestors?

Where did they live?

What kind of work did they do?

Historically, what happened during their lifetimes?

What major events happened to them?

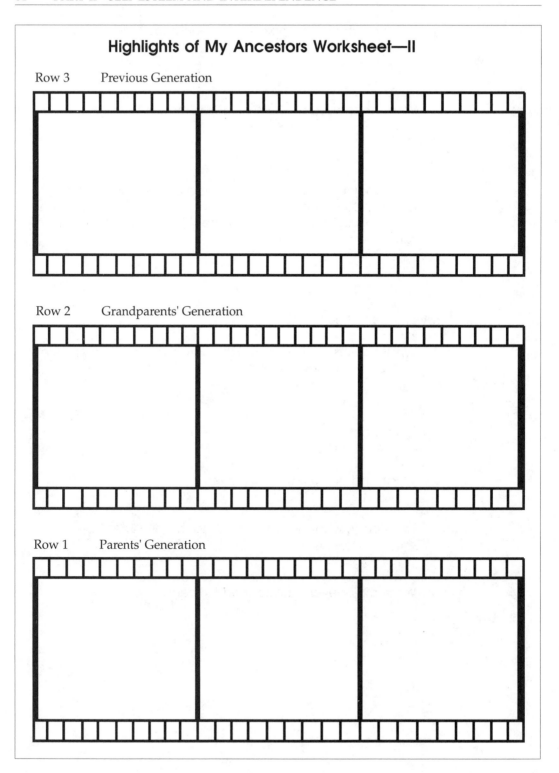

Highlights of My Ancestors Worksheet—II

Row 3   Previous Generation

Row 2   Grandparents' Generation

Row 1   Parents' Generation

21 The Joy of Eating

*F*ood is the most primitive form of comfort.

—Sheilah Graham

A good cook is like a sorceress
who dispenses happiness.

—Elsa Schiaparelli

Background

Food is at the heart of most cultures. It often embodies the heritage of a race, traces historical and geographic influences over time, and reflects a style, an aesthetic, and the taste—literally as well as figuratively—of a particular culture. It is hard to imagine Italians without pasta, Mexicans without tortillas, Chinese without rice, or Americans without apple pie.

American food, however, is certainly more than just apple pie. Many foods that are considered American have origins that can be traced to other lands. Peanuts came from South America, for instance. Other examples are potatoes which come from the Andes via Ireland, or oranges, picked in Asia, traded to Africa and the Middle East by Arabs, and brought here from the Mediterranean countries.

Pumpkin pie blends the English concept of pie with Native American pumpkin and Asian spices like cinnamon and nutmeg. "Puffed" cereal also originated in colonial days, when English housewives served Native American popcorn with sugar and cream for breakfast.

American food customs are derived from all parts of the word: Consider Chinese-style chicken salad, Cajun-spiced French fries, teriyaki hamburgers, and Mexican pizza. Today's grocery stores are stocked with the ingredients necessary to prepare every type of food imaginable.

Purpose

This activity helps students identify with their cultural roots and take pride in its culinary contributions.

Procedure

1. Ask students to identify the person at home who cooks their favorite meal.

2. Give students the assignment of interviewing this person to find out as much as possible about the food they enjoy.

Either prepare a list of questions in advance and hand these out to the students as a way of structuring the interview, or, together with the students, brainstorm possible questions to ask such as:

"How long have you been cooking this type of food?"
"How did you learn how to prepare it?"
"How long has the recipe been in the family?"
"How did our people come to this type of cooking?"

Note: You may want to expand this activity to have students go to the library to do more research on how food traditions evolved in their culture.

3. Have students bring in a copy of the recipe for their favorite meal. Students could also bring in a photograph of their favorite meal or do an illustration of part of the recipe.

4. Make copies of the students' recipes and illustrations and bind these together into booklets so that every student has a complete set of recipes.

Note: As a class project, these recipe books could be sold to raise money to cover the cost of duplicating and binding. Profits could be used to help finance a field trip or some other activity. (See "Team Problem Solving," Activity 61, for a possible way of structuring this.)

Also, this "business venture" could be used to teach math concepts.

If feasible, students could actually prepare some of the recipes in class, or a Multicultural Food Fair or potluck supper could be held where family members are invited to bring in dishes to share with each other. Back-to-School Night, holiday celebrations, or graduation are particular good times for such an activity.

When snacks are made available to students, consider ways of providing nutritious food reflective of many cultures.

22 My Own Culture

*O*ur mothers and grandmothers, some of them;
moving to music not yet written.

—Alice Walker

Background*

Many cultures have their own folklore regarding the importance of a new year, with particular customs that are intended to ensure good fortune, prosperity, happiness, and longevity.

Ecuadorian New Year is celebrated on December 31 by families creating dolls out of old rags representing the old year. On New Year's Eve, the figures are placed on decorated chairs. Everyone pins their resolutions for the New Year on these dolls as the children sing and dance. At midnight the figures are removed as the New Year begins.

Chinese New Year occurs later in January or in February. Families gather together, houses are cleaned, tools repaired, clothes mended, and debts paid—all symbolic of completing the past to get ready for a new beginning. Bright red, the color of good fortune, is seen everywhere. Evil spirits are scared away by firecrackers and the Dancing Dragon, who brings good wishes.

Vietnamese New Year (Tet) is in the spring. Everything and everyone is prepared for the New Year. As with the Chinese, houses are repainted, furniture is cleaned, and new clothes are worn. At midnight, families go to the temple to give thanks. Flowers and branches from fruit trees are used to symbolize prosperity and happiness. People visit friends, give gifts, and feast during this spring festival of reunion and renewal.

Some **Native American** tribes celebrated their New Year during the summer, in late July or early August, when the corn was ripe and the fruits and vegetables were ready to eat. At this time, family ties were renewed, new law's were made, past mistakes were forgiven, and all the people of the tribe reflected on the importance of getting along together. Old fires were put out, new ones were lighted, and the Green Corn Dance was celebrated.

Jewish New Year (Rosh Hashanah), in the fall, is a serious holy day that is greeted with a quiet and solemn heart. Sweet foods are served, signifying a sweet new year ahead.

---

*The background information was adapted from *Children of the Rainbow—First Grade,* Board of Education of the City of New York, 1991, and "Ring in the New Year with Old Customs" by Marina Cianci in the *San Francisco Chronicle,* December 30, 1992.

Many other cultures have New Year customs that involve food as part of the symbolism:

- In Japan, *toshikoshi soba* ("year crossover") noodles are eaten for wealth and long life.

- The Portuguese eat a dozen raisins or pomegranate seeds—good luck for each month of the year—and the Spanish use grapes for the same purpose.

- An Italian custom is eating lentils, symbolizing money, and *cotechino* (a type of pork sausage), symbolizing richness.

- The Dutch have their *oliebollen*—doughnuts—and Greeks have their *vasilopita*—a wreath of decorated sweet bread with a golden coin hidden inside for good fortune.

- In the Southern United States, eating rice and black-eyed peas on New Year's Day is thought to bring good luck.

- And, of course, the French contributed the tradition of celebrating with champagne.

Purpose

This activity will help students appreciate what constitutes a culture and will engender a greater sense of pride in their culture.

Procedure

1. Write the word *culture* on the board and ask students to brainstorm what they think of when they think of culture. You may need to do some coaching, such as:

   Teacher: When I say "Chinese culture," what do you think of?

   Student: Chinese food.

   Teacher: Good. So food is one aspect of culture.

   Teacher: What do you think of when I say "Mexican"?

   Student: Mariachi band.

   Teacher: So, music and dance are part of culture. Good.

   Teacher: How about French culture?

   Student: A beret or "Oui, oui."

Teacher: Yes, clothes and language are part of culture.

Teacher: What do you think of when I say "Russia"?

Student: Communism.

Teacher: Forms of government and historical events also make up a country's culture.

2. Make the point that one way of understanding *culture* is to see it as the knowledge, ideas, and skills that enable a group of people to survive in their environment. All people have essentially the same basic human needs and wants. How these needs are fulfilled in the context of the group's environment is what constitutes culture.

3. Ask the students to name some things they think all human beings need in order to survive. Record their answers on the board or on butcher paper. "Food," "clothing," "shelter" are typical responses. Refer back to the earlier set of questions for other ideas, such as language, art, and government. Continue to ask probing questions to help students identify other needs such as: love, family, and friendship; work and the economy; the meaning of life and religion.

4. Hand out the My Culture Worksheet and have the students fill it out for their own culture. If their heritage is multicultural, they may use a separate sheet for each culture or combine aspects from all their cultures on the same sheet. Fill one out yourself and use it as a sample. Answer any questions the students might have. For some of the answers, the students may need to refer back to their cultural group's heritage for unique expressions of, for example, clothing and shelter.

5. Have students share the answers on their worksheets in pairs or small groups.

6. End the activity with a full-class discussion regarding similarities and variations of the different cultures. You can make a chart on the board or on butcher paper to help focus the discussion.

Human Need	German	Korean	Navajo	Filipino
Food				
Clothing				
Shelter				
Language				
Music/Art/Dance				
Family				
Other				

My Culture Worksheet

Name _____   Cultural Groups _____

Food _____

_____

_____

Clothing _____

_____

_____

Shelter _____

_____

_____

Language _____

_____

_____

Music/Art/Dance _____

_____

_____

Customs/Traditions Related to Family _____

_____

_____

Other Unique Characteristics _____

_____

_____

23 The Cultures We Are

*My race is a line that stretches across ocean
and time to link me to the shrines
where my grandmother was raised.*

—Kesaya E. Noda

Purpose

This can done in your classroom or as a schoolwide activity. It is meant to celebrate all the various cultures in your school community, and to increase awareness and understanding of these cultures.

Procedure

1. Begin this activity by reading to your class, *Angel Child, Dragon Child* by Michelle Maria Surat. This delightful book is about a Vietnamese child who at first is teased for being different but whose story eventually inspires a new sense of community at her school.

2. Brainstorm with your students any questions they have that they would like to ask someone from a different culture. Emphasize that respect for all people of all cultures is essential. The previous activity contains some possible areas to explore. Also consider:

   "What customs are particular to your culture?"

   - at the birth of a child
   - when someone dies
   - at weddings
   - at birthdays
   - during holidays
   - rites of passage (*bar mitzvah*, confirmation, etc.)

   "What foods are native to your culture?"

   "What are the common characteristics of the artwork created by people in your culture?"

   "What type of music is usually played at family gatherings?"

   "Are there particular colors that are frequently used in the clothing worn by people in your culture?"

   "What artifacts and crafts are enjoyed by people in your culture?"

"What is your culture's attitude toward its elders?"

"What rules of conduct determine acceptance or rejection in your culture?"

"How important is religion/spirituality in your culture?"

"How is success defined in your culture?"

"Who are your culture's heroes and heroines?"

Some student-generated questions were:

"Are your parents strict or easy?"

"Where do you get your spending money? Do you get an allowance? How much?"

"Do your parents expect you to go to college?"

"Are you likely to work in your family's business?"

"Can you pick your own clothes?"

3. Select the seven questions that have the most interest for the class, and ask the students to bring these home to discuss with their families. Pick a date by which all students will bring in their answers.

You may want to put the questions onto a worksheet to make it easier for the students. You probably also will want to inform the families in advance of the assignment so that they will understand its purpose and won't feel that the school is prying into their family background.

4. Plan with your students how you will share this information with each other or with the entire school. Here are some suggestions:

- Cut construction paper into the shape of balloons. Print the name of the culture and one fact about it on each side of the paper and suspend them all from the ceiling with string so that they hang at student eye level—a visual celebration of cultural diversity.
- Print a Multicultural Newsletter with a separate page for each culture containing all the facts collected by the students from that particular culture. Students could illustrate the pages of the newsletter with culturally-related drawings.
- Post a large map of the world and highlight the countries of origin represented by your students. Use Post-it® notes to display facts about the cultures of the countries.
- Have your class publish "Our Geography Book" or "Our History Book," where the facts about the various cultures can be gathered in a textbook-like fashion. Additional research could be done to expand the knowledge of each culture.
- Students could design quizzes that they could give to their classmates on each culture.

5. Conclude this activity with a class discussion about what the students learned. Explore with them the idea that one's culture often influences family patterns, and yet no one family can represent an entire culture. Families, like individuals, are unique.

24   Sense Us

This country is great because of its accommodations with diversity. The richness of the diversity of this country is a treasure and it's a constant challenge to remain tolerant and respectful of one another.
—Ruth Bader Ginsburg

Background

In 1790, when the first U.S. census was conducted, the race classifications were white, slave, and other. By 1870, the categories had evolved to include white, colored (black), colored (mulattos), Chinese, and Indian. Two decades later, the distinctions among blacks became more detailed: blacks, mulattos (those with three-eights to five-eighths "black blood"), quadroons (those with one-quarter black blood), and octoroons (those with one-eighth black blood). This "blood" ratio was later dropped; by 1930, anyone of mixed black and white heritage was put in the "Negro" category.

The current racial and ethnic categories are white, black, Asian/Pacific Islander, American Indian, Hispanic, and other. When told to pick one box, however, people of multiracial backgrounds are faced with a dilemma. As interracial marriages increase—from 310,000 in 1970 to 1.2 million in 1992 (a 365 percent jump)—hundreds of thousands of multiracial children cannot officially claim an identity of their own. Should they pick one parent over the other, check the "other" box, check more than one box—or should the form itself be changed? This is the challenge for your students to address.*

*Statistics contained in the background material for this activity come from "Census Misses the Mark on Race" by Thaai Walker, *San Francisco Chronicle*, July 26, 1993.

Purpose

The purpose of this activity is to validate students who are multiracial or multiethnic by raising issues regarding society's view of people who cross racial lines. By the way, it was not until 1967 that the last laws barring interracial marriages were fully repealed.

Procedure

1. Discuss with your students the idea of doing a census, what purpose it serves, and the possible reasons for including race categories. For example, the Voting Rights Act requires that minorities have proportional representation in local government and legislation. So, information regarding the ethnic makeup of the population is essential to ensuring that all people are appropriately represented.

2. Hand out the Sense Us Worksheet and ask the students first to check the box that best describes their racial makeup.

3. Next, explain that each category may be made up of specific subgroups: Hispanic may include Mexican, Puerto Rican, Cuban, and so forth; Asian might include Korean, Vietnamese, and Taiwanese, as well as Chinese and Japanese; white may include any number of European nationalities; and so forth.

   Have students fill in their cultural makeup in greater detail and indicate the relative percentages.

4. Now, demonstrate how to make a pie chart and have the students draw one that reflects their cultural heritage.

5. You may want to extend this activity to the development of a census of the entire class by calculating the data on each student in a composite chart.

6. Students could also do a schoolwide census by distributing the worksheets to each classroom and compiling the data to form a composite pie chart for the entire student body.

7. In discussing the activity with the students afterwards, make reference to the multiracial category as one that is not included on the actual U.S. census. Ask them how they would feel if they could choose only one of the other boxes.

Sense Us Worksheet

Please check the appropriate box:

- ❏ White _____ _____ %
- ❏ Black _____ _____ %
- ❏ Asian/Pacific Islander _____ _____ %
- ❏ American Indian _____ _____ %
- ❏ Hispanic _____ _____ %
- ❏ Other race _____ _____ %
- ❏ Multirace _____ _____ %

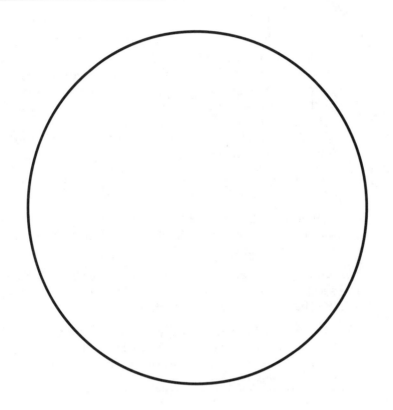

Chapter 3—Suggested Student Readings

Brown, Tricia. *Chinese New Year.* New York: Henry Holt, 1987.

Clifton, Lucille. *The Lucky Stone.* New York: Delacorte, 1979.

Dr. Seuss. *Are You My Mother?* New York: Random House, 1960.

Feeling, Muriel. *Jambo Means Hello.* New York: Dial, 1974.

Feeling, Muriel. *Zamani Goes to Market.* New York: Seabury Press, 1970.

Friedman, Ina R. *How My Parents Learned to Eat.* Boston: Houghton Mifflin, 1984.

Greenfield, Eloise. *Talk about a Family.* New York: Lippincott, 1978.

Robles, Al. *Looking for Ifugao Mountain.* San Francisco: Children's Book Press, 1977.

San Souci, Robert D., & Stephen T. Johnson. *The Samurai's Daughter.* New York: Dial, 1992.

Senfozo, Mary. *Welcome Roberto! Bienvenido Roberto!* Chicago: Follett, 1969.

Simon, Norma. *All Kinds of Families.* Neil, IL: A. Whitman 1976.

Sullivan, Charles. *Children of Promise.* New York: Harry N. Abrams, 1991.

Surat, Michelle Maria. *Angel Child, Dragon Child.* New York: Scholastic, 1983.

Tax, Meredith. *Families.* Boston: Little, Brown, 1981.

Sharing and Support

Celebrating Diversity

*A*merica is not like a blanket—one piece of
unbroken cloth, the same color, the same texture,
the same size. America is more like a quilt—many
pieces, many colors, many sizes, all woven
and held together by a common thread.
—Jesse Jackson

Introduction

I always wanted to be somebody. If I make it,
it's half because I was game enough to take a lot of
punishment along the way and half because there were
a lot of people who cared enough to help me.
—Althea Gibson

"O Hawk, see what making friends has meant! Thanks to these good friends
you sent, each one of us is safe and sound. What better help could ever be
found?"

Knowing the importance of friends, the female Hawk agreed to marry the
male Hawk on the condition that he make some friends. She suggested a Lion—
the king of the beasts who lives in the fields to the north, an Osprey—the king of
the birds who lives on the eastern shore, and the great Tortoise who dwells on
the island in the middle of the lake.

One day when the Hawk's children were threatened by some country folk
who came to the forest hunting for food, each of the friends came to help. The

Osprey put out the fire that was smoking the birds out of the tree. The Tortoise pulled the people into the deep water away from the birds. The Lion frightened them away.

The Hawks and their friends remained faithful to each other for the rest of their lives.*

This chapter is about making and keeping friends. It helps students define what makes a good friend and gives them the tools to be good friends themselves. The intent is for young people to base their friendships on qualities such as "caring," "supportive," and "fun," rather than by race, creed, or color.

Multicultural Support Teams are formed to encourage students to relate to their classmates from other cultures and learn the benefits of having friends from diverse backgrounds.

25 That's What Friends Are For

Yes'm, old friends is always best, 'less you can catch a new one that's fit to make an old one out of.
—Sarah Orne Jewett

There are deep sorrows and killing cares in life, but the encouragement and love of friends were given us to make all difficulties bearable.
—John Oliver Hobbes

Purpose

Knowledge of oneself occurs in a social context. Someone who is totally isolated would not receive the feedback necessary to make the important distinctions that expand one's sense of self. To identify oneself as tall or short, light or dark, serious or jovial, requires the presence of others with whom to compare and contrast.

Acceptance by others—a sense of belonging—is essential to healthy self-esteem.

Many adults—fearing the unknown—tend to associate with others who are similar to themselves in terms of nationality, religion, economic class,

*The Value of Friends: A Jataka Tale, illustrated by Eric Meller (Oakland, CA: Dharma Press, 1990).

and so forth. This "birds of a feather" syndrome may serve to maintain one's personal comfort level, but it also robs us of the opportunity to experience the cultural richness that diversity provides.

This activity is meant to help our children appreciate what attributes are important in friends so that they can be good friends themselves and select friends on the basis of true values rather than surface similarities.

Materials

one copy of the Friends Are For Worksheet per student (reproduced on cardboard if possible)

index cards or Post-it® notes, twelve per student

Procedure

1. Give each student a copy of the Friends Are For Worksheet and twelve index cards or Post-it® Notes.

2. Engage the students in a discussion of friendship and have them brainstorm what they like in a friend. Record these qualities on the board for all the students to see. Be nonjudgmental—record all comments students offer.

   You may want to add some of your own if you feel that the student-generated list needs to be expanded. Avoid setting up a situation where the students feel your answers are better than theirs.

   To increase students' awareness of cultural stereotypes and peer pressure, you can raise these issues by adding items such as: "same sneakers as mine," "same hair style as mine," "same skin color as mine," "same religion as mine," and so forth.

3. Now, instruct the students to pick the top six qualities that they feel are important in a good friend. Have them write one quality on each card.

4. Next, tell them to place the cards in order on their worksheet, with the quality in space 1 being the most important, and so forth.

5. When they are finished placing all six cards in the appropriate spaces, ask for their attention. In order to check if, in fact, the most important qualities have been selected, propose the following scenario:

   "Imagine that from all your friends you had to choose one to join you and your family on a cross-country car trip. Since you will be in a car most of the time, the friend you pick will be the person with whom you will spend all your time."

Are there any other qualities you would want this person to have that we did not already mention?

6. Put on the board any additional thoughts the students have.

7. Invite them to consider if these newly identified qualities are more important than the six they already put on their chart. If so, they should rearrange their cards to accommodate these.

8. Here is another scenario to consider:

> "Some of you may have heard of the disease alopecia areata, which causes all of one's hair to fall out. Bob Samuelson, one of the athletes in the 1992 Summer Olympics, had it and all of his teammates shaved their heads in support of him.
>
> "What if you discovered that you had this disease? How might it change your life, and what types of friends would you want to have around you?"

9. Once again, add any other words to the list on the board, and have the students make any changes in their charts. They should now have a fairly clear sense of what matters to them in terms of friendship.

10. Ask the students to get into small groups of five or six and share with each other the qualities they selected as most important in friends.

11. Bring the students together and read with them *That's What Friends Are For* by Carol Adorjan (New York: Scholastic, 1990).

Friends Are For Worksheet

①

②

③

④

⑤

⑥

26 What Kind of Friend Am I?

*You can hardly make a friend in a year,
but you can lose one in an hour.*

—Chinese Proverb

Purpose

The activity is a follow-up to the previous one. It supports students in developing the skills necessary to be a good friend.

Materials

charts and cards from Activity 25, "That's What Friends Are For"

Procedure

Review with your students the lessons learned during the previous lesson on friendship.

1. Distribute copies of the What Kind of Friend Am I? Worksheet, and help students fill it out as follows:

   "Start with the quality you identified as being the most important one for a good friend to have. Write this at the top of the page."

   "Now, list as many ways you can think of in which someone shows that they have this quality. For example, if the quality is kindness, then friends show kindness by sharing things with you, saying nice things about you, inviting you to do things with them, listening to your problems, and so forth."

   "Finally, think about how good a friend you are. To what extent do you have this quality? How often do you do the Acts of Friendship you identified?"

   "Pick at least one thing you can do more often to be a better friend and write it on the 'I promise to' line."

   "Sign the page to show that you mean it."

2. Invite the students to get into small groups and share their answers.

3. During the course of the next few days, find opportunities to reinforce this lesson. Ask students to review their worksheets and report on progress.

4. You may repeat this exercise in a week or two using the second and third highest friendship qualities that the students selected.

Alternative Version Procedure

1. Review with your students the lessons learned during the previous lesson on friendship.

2. Ask each student to say aloud what he or she selected as the most important quality of a friend, and list these qualities on the chalkboard or butcher paper.

3. Identify the six most frequently mentioned qualities of a friend and underline them.

4. Divide the class into six Expert Groups and have each group take one of the most frequently mentioned qualities of friends. Ask them to list as many ways as they can think of for people to show that they have this quality. The same What Kind of Friend Am I? Worksheet can be used to record each group's answers.

5. Next, have one student from each of these expert groups form a new group. Ask each expert to share with their new teammates the Acts of Friendship that their group identified.

6. Focus on one of the following themes each day for the next week or so:

   - Discuss the Acts of Friendship each morning, and ask the students to promise which of these they will practice today.
   - Throughout the day—after recess, after lunch, and so forth— check in with the students to see how well they're doing.
   - At the end of the day, or at some other appropriate time, read a story to the students that has a character who models some of the friendship characteristics they identified. Have the students discuss the story, talking about what they liked about the character, and so forth.

What Kind of Friend Am I? Worksheet

Friendship Quality

_____

Acts of Friendship

_____

_____

_____

_____

_____

_____

_____

I Promise to

_____

_____

_____

_____

_____

_____

_____

_____
Name

27 Promises to Keep

Seeing's believing, but feeling is God's own truth.
—Irish Proverb

Purpose

The purpose of this activity is to develop a classroom community based on shared values regarding friendship and respect.

Procedure

1. Prepare yourself or have each student Expert Group prepare a chart of the Friendship Qualities and Acts of Friendship developed in the previous activity.

2. Review the lists with the class to decide which of the items could relate to the class as a whole.

   For example, if the Friendship Quality is "kindness" and a related Act of Friendship is "listening," then the class application could be "listen when someone else is speaking."

3. If the Acts of Friendship as written do not cover all the important aspects of a safe and supportive classroom environment, you may want to do some coaching, asking questions such as:

   "What would need to happen in the classroom so everyone feels supported and included?"

   "What would need to happen in the classroom so everyone can hear directions?"

   "What agreement would we need to make in order for us to start class together so that no one misses anything and others aren't kept waiting for students who aren't here?"

4. Encourage students to say what they think. Accept their comments without evaluation, and use their wording as much as possible.

5. When all the classroom-related Acts of Friendship have been identi- fied, work with the students to eliminate duplications, combine similar items, and reduce the total number to a manageable length. Seven items is probably as many as can be remembered.

6. Discuss with the students the idea of making an agreement or a promise. Ask them if they would be willing to promise to keep these

agreements in order to have the classroom be safe and workable for everyone.

7. Write the final list of Classroom Agreements on a large poster for all the students to sign, or on individual sheets such as the Classroom Agreements Worksheet.

   You may want to send a copy home to the students' parents and guardians to inform them of their children's agreements. Having parents sign and return them is a way of ensuring that they got the information.

Sample Agreements

- Listen when someone else is speaking.
- Be on time.
- Be prepared.
- Follow instructions.
- Be nice to myself and to each other.
- Work to the best of my ability.
- Maintain confidentiality. (What is shared in the classroom stays in the classroom.)

Common Challenges

When a student does not follow an agreement, ask the student if he or she is aware of breaking an agreement and, if so, which one. The student usually knows. Once the broken agreement is acknowledged, ask if he or she is willing to recommit to keeping the promise. If the student says yes, restate the promise and acknowledge the importance of being responsible for keeping one's word.

If the student says no, discuss the issue until you and he or she reach a new agreement. The key here is not to make the breaking of the guideline an issue that requires punitive action. Be firm and clear, but not confrontational. When the guidelines are self-enforced, there is a much higher level of cooperation from all students.

Peer coaching may be used to support students in keeping their agreements. Class meetings—described in the next activity—are a good place to discuss Classroom Agreements.

Classroom Agreements Worksheet

The following list of Classroom Agreements were identified by our class.

_____

_____

_____

_____

_____

_____

_____

I know what these agreements mean and promise to keep them.

_____   _____

Student Signature   Date

28 My Circle of Friends

The world is round and the place which may seem like the end may also be only the beginning.
—Ivy Baker Priest

Purpose

This activity is intended to help you establish a regular routine of class meetings or sharing sessions that can be used on an ongoing basis to deepen students' sense of belonging and to deal with specific issues that arise in most classrooms.

During this structured time, students will learn to:

• Share their feelings in a responsible manner

• Listen to others with greater patience and compassion

- Appreciate that they are not alone in dealing with difficult situations

- Cope with problems in more effective ways by hearing how others have resolved similar issues.

As their teacher, you will increase your understanding of your students and their thoughts, feelings, desires, fears, and challenges, which will better prepare you to help them academically and socially.

Procedure

1. Brainstorm with your students objects or gestures that connote friendship in different cultures. Some examples follow:

Objects	*Gestures*
• friendship ring	• handshake
• yellow rose	• high five
• lei (Hawaiian)	• American Sign Language (ASL) gesture for "I Love You"
• peace pipe/talking stick (Native American)	
• teddy bear	• peace sign
	• bowing (Japanese)
	• "Nameste" (Hindu)

2. Use one of these objects or gestures as a way of focusing the students. Bring the students into a full circle so that everyone can see everyone else. Whoever is holding the object is the center of attention. It is this person's turn to share while everyone else listens.

   The object is passed around the circle until everyone has had a chance to speak.

   Students are always welcome to pass if they have nothing to say at this time.

3. Remind students of the classroom agreements, especially those that are relevant to this activity.

   It is, of course, strongly desirable that all members of the class physically participate in the circle. In rare instances, however, when an individual student is unwilling to commit to keeping the agreements during Circle Time, you may have him or her sit outside the circle. Give an assignment that can be done quietly at a desk. The task might be related to the topic that is being discussed by the students in the circle. For example, a topic for Circle Time could be, "Share about a time you did something nice for someone," which could also be a theme for an essay or drawing that a student could work on outside the circle. A student outside the circle can choose to join the group by recommitting to the class agreements.

4. It is recommended that you do a Circle of Friends on a frequent basis—perhaps daily, at least once per week. The length of activity depends on how much time is available, as well as on the age and maturity of your students and the level of interest in the particular topic.

   If time runs out before every student has had a chance to share, pick up next time where you left off. You can also put a time limit on each student's sharing. For example, each student might say just one word to describe how he or she feels this morning, or each student might get one minute to share.

   Circle time may also be done in small groups rather than as a full class. The next activity will provide guidelines for how to set up these student support groups.

5. Circle of Friends may be used to address particular issues such as:

   - classroom agreements
   - feelings related to an upcoming test
   - an incident in the playground
   - excessive teasing of a particular student or group
   - planning a field trip
   - loss of a major athletic event
   - a social, political, or community issue that is getting a lot of attention
   - loss of a pet
   - death of a schoolmate

6. Circle time can also be a regularly scheduled part of the classroom program. For example:

   - in the morning, to focus the students on plans for the day
   - after lunch, to refocus for the afternoon
   - at the end of the day, to review and bring closure to the day's events
   - as a part of certain subjects, to discuss feelings about a story, film, or lesson

7. Possible topics for Circle of Friends—clustered around the themes of this book—include:

   - Identity

     —something I like about myself _____

     —something I like about being _____
       (African-American, Hispanic, Jewish, Native American, Vietnamese, etc.)

     —something that makes me special

- Belonging
  - —things I do to be a good friend
  - —what I like about my friends
  - —a time when I was new and didn't know how to meet friends
  - —a time someone helped me feel like I belonged
  - —a time when I trusted someone and they came through
  - —a time when I trusted someone and they let me down
- Achievement
  - —a goal I achieved recently
  - —something I intend to achieve this year
  - —a successful person I admire
  - —the best school-related achievement I ever got and how I earned it
  - —other areas of my life where I feel successful (sports, musical talent, friends, at home, etc.)

29   Everyone Belongs

It really boils down to this: that all life is interrelated.
We are all caught in an inescapable network
of mutuality, tied into a single garment of destiny.
Whatever affects one directly, affects all indirectly.
—Martin Luther King, Jr.

Purpose

In this activity, students will appreciate that everyone belongs, everyone is needed, and everyone has a contribution to make. Students will also recognize the importance of working together as a team to accomplish a common goal. They will become aware of the relationship between personal success and group or team success, and will realize that when they shift from personal self-interest to concern for the needs of others, their own needs get taken care of in the process.

Note: In advance, prepare sets of broken square puzzles as diagrammed.

Procedure

1. Divide the class into groups of five students. (If there are extra students, have them function as "observers." The observer's job is to watch the process, notice how the team approaches putting together the puzzle, and be prepared to report during the debriefing.)

2. Tell them: "The purpose of this activity is for you to experience the interrelationship of everyone and the connection between personal success and group success. The goal of this activity is for each of you to put together a square that is equal in size to the square of everyone else on your team."

   "The operating instructions are as follows:

   - Players may not talk, point, or communicate in any way with the other people in the group.
   - Players may give pieces to other participants but may not just take pieces from another person.
   - Players may not throw their pieces into the center for others to take; they must give the pieces directly to an individual.
   - Players may give away pieces to their puzzle, even after they have already formed a square."

   In order for this game to work, each player must make a commitment to the purpose, goal, and operating instructions. Ask, "Is there anyone not willing to follow the operating instructions?" (Answer questions or concerns. If there are some unwilling to participate, assign these students as observers.) Tell them, "Those of you who are observers are to watch the process, notice how the team approaches putting the puzzles together, and be prepared to report back to us."

3. Allow enough time for each group to complete the activity. Ask groups who are finished to wait quietly until the others are done. Let the students who are finished talk among themselves about their experience of the activity. You might also ask them to give clues to the groups who are still working on the puzzle, without revealing too much and spoiling the fun of discovery.

4. Bring the class together to debrief:

   "What worked?"

   "What got in the way of success?"

   "Based on this experience, what would you say is important for individual success and group success?"

   (Responses to the last question can be written on the board under the heading "Guidelines for Individual and Group Success.")

5. You may want to make the following concluding remarks:

> "This exercise serves as a model for how we can create a classroom, school, and society where everybody wins. Recognizing that there is no scarcity, there are no missing pieces, we realize that the universe already has everything that any of us could need or want.
>
> We each have a contribution to make to the whole. We can each look at what other people need and give what we have to give. We can be open to what other people have contributed to us. Then, like magic, it all comes together.
>
> What is needed is a commitment to our own personal success and also a commitment to contribute to the success of everyone else in the class."

Supplementary Activity

A nice way to end this activity is to read *Horton Hears a Who* by Dr. Seuss (New York: Random House, 1954) to the class. This delightful book stresses this same theme—that everyone's contribution is important, that we are all indispensable pieces to the overall puzzle.

Everyone Belongs Puzzle Pieces

To make the puzzle pieces for this activity, use poster board or heavy coated paper. For each group of five or six students, cut five 6-inch squares. Using the following patterns, cut each of the squares into pieces. (Note: All the A's are the same size.)

Now, in order to mix the pieces up, put them in envelopes as follows:

Envelope A: pieces I, H, E   Envelope B: A, A, A, C
Envelope C: pieces A, J   Envelope D: D, F
Envelope E: pieces G, B, F, C

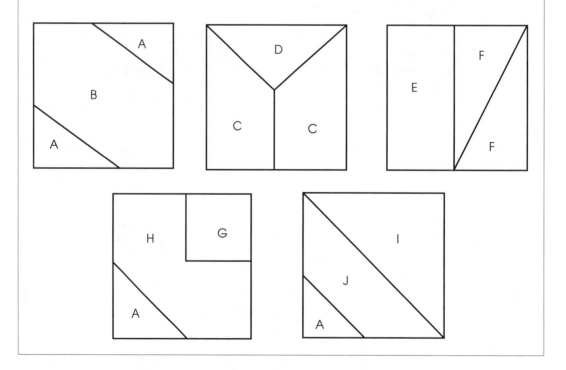

30 Multicultural Support Teams

*E*ach friend represents a world in us, a world
possibly not born until they arrive, and it is only
by this meeting that a new world is born.

—Anais Nin

Purpose

The activities at the beginning of this section are designed to create a
classroom where all students feel included as part of the full group.

Allowing students to work in smaller groups will help deepen their
level of interaction and provide greater opportunity for every student—
especially the shy, reticent child—to express him- or herself more freely.

Since we want to celebrate diversity and encourage an appreciation for
students from various cultures, this activity deliberately divides the students
into support teams that are as multicultural as the makeup of your class
allows. Read through the procedure first to make sure it is appropriate for
your class given the number of ethnic groups represented by your students.
For alternative ways of establishing Multicultural Support Teams, see the
variations at the end of this activity.

Procedure

Part I

1. Get a large map of the world or a globe and divide it into six roughly
   equal parts. When deciding how to section off the map, consider the
   nationalities represented by your students, because you will want
   students to represent each of the six sections.

2. Post the numbers 1 through 6 in distinct places in your classroom
   where students have room to stand during the process.

3. Show the map to the students, correlating the number of each section
   of the map with the numbers placed around the room.

   With your students, identify the various countries contained in
   each section. Ask the students to associate their own cultural heritage
   with a particular country or part of the world, and consider where in
   the room they will go to stand when it is time.

   Answer any questions that students have about the country to
   which they might feel connected. Students whose ancestry belongs to

more than one part of the world may choose the one with which they most identify.

4. Now have the students move to the part of the room that represents their part of the map.

Do your best to even out the groups wherever possible. You may have some sections of the globe well represented and others not reflected at all by students in your class.

5. To end the first part of the activity, have the students get into a circle with those who are from the same part of the world.

Have them discuss aspects of their culture and ancestry that they have in common.

Some discussion topics include:

"What country in this region does your family come from?"
"What language is spoken there?"
"Do you and/or members of your family speak this language?"
"What kind of food is eaten in this country?"
"Do you and your family still eat this type of food at home?"
"When did your family leave this country and come to America?"
"What were the reasons that your family came to America?"

Part II

1. Next, we want to move the students into Multicultural Support Teams by having students from each of the regional groups get together with students from other regions.

Within each group, have the students count off from 1 to 5. All the "1's" then get together to form a new team. So do the "2's", "3's", and so forth.

If there are fewer than five students in any group, ask them to wait until the teams are formed in case the higher numbers have fewer students.

For the same reason, if a group has more than five students, have the first five form their new teams and let the others wait.

The intended result is to have teams of five or six students, with each team as culturally diverse as possible.

2. Once the teams are formed, have the students gather into a circle to spend some time getting to know each other and discussing their countries of origin. Some of the discussion topics from Part I would also be appropriate here.

You could also allow students to ask each other questions about themselves, their families, and their culture.

Team agreements that would support this process are:

- Students should only ask questions that they themselves would be willing to answer.
- They should ask questions that are likely to support their teammates in feeling proud rather than embarrassed.
- Students are always welcome to pass.

3. Multicultural Support Teams may be used in the same ways as Circle of Friends—on an ongoing basis as well as to deal with specific issues. The same topics would work, and less time would be needed.

4. The Classroom Agreements used for Circle of Friends should apply equally well here. Student Support Teams are welcome to make their own agreements, provided everyone on the team is willing to promise to keep them, and provided they are not in conflict with the rest of the class agreements.

5. In addition to expanding multicultural awareness and promoting feelings of belonging, Student Support Teams can also be used to help students achieve academically.

   Student teams can work together:

   - as cooperative learning units on school-related projects
   - to follow up with each other on homework and other academic goals
   - to ensure that if a student is absent, he or she gets caught up on the assignments
   - to share different learning styles and study skills to help others in their group learn new strategies for success
   - as discussion groups to integrate key points of a lesson, to evaluate what they learned and what they still don't understand, and to bring closure to a lesson.

6. The Multicultural Support Teams may be used throughout the school year.

   Students often resist the idea at first, especially if their friends are on other teams. Be patient and allow enough time for the students to build relationships with their teammates.

   If you decide to change the makeup of the groups at the end of a month or semester, keep in mind the aim of celebrating diversity.

   Children are not very different from adults where group dynamics are concerned. Virtually all teams go through four stages—forming, storming, transforming, and performing. As the word *storming* implies, challenges arise that will need to be resolved. Student Support Teams provide many opportunities to practice group problem-solving techniques. Making and keeping agreements is one way to settle disputes. "Conflict Management" (Activity 63) is another structured approach.

You may also want to introduce the communication activity, "SHARE to Show You Care" (Activity 57), at this time if you feel the students need to develop their listening skills.

Variation I

In situations where your class will not divide evenly into cultural teams or when students are not likely to know the answers to these questions, you could set this up as a research project. For Part I of the activity, students could choose what group they want to join and study the heritage of this culture in order to answer the questions. They could then move into Part II.

Variation II

The process of clustering students into Multicultural Support Teams could be simplified by your assigning them to groups based on their cultural background. You would want to explain to them the purpose of the grouping and be prepared to deal with some students complaining about their assignment.

31 Colors of the Rainbow

*Just people from everywhere are related
to me by blood and so that's why I say
I'm a multicultural event. . . . It's beautiful,
it's a rainbow. . . . It reflects light. . . .*

—Paula Gunn Allen

Purpose

The rainbow has been used as a metaphor for the beauty of cultural diversity. Each color has its own identity and value and they come together to create a multihued wonder of nature.

The purpose of this activity is to introduce this concept to students and to have them appreciate their place—and the place of everyone else—in the wonder of nature that is humanity.

Materials

large sheets of butcher paper—one for each Student Multicultural Support Team

crayons or colored markers, a set for each team that includes the colors of the rainbow

Procedure

1. Introduce the idea of rainbows to students by:

   • asking how many students have actually seen a rainbow
   • asking students to name the colors of the rainbow
   • showing photographs or reading a book on the subject such as *The Storm Book* by Charlotte Zolotow (New York: HarperCollins, 1989)

2. Link the idea of a rainbow with the value of cultural diversity.

3. Let the students know that they will be making a rainbow with the members of their Support Team.

4. Distribute paper and crayons to the student teams.

   Instruct the students to decide from among themselves which student will use which color of the rainbow.

5. Each student takes a turn—starting with the student who has the red crayon and continuing through the colors of the rainbow: red, orange, yellow, green, blue, violet.

   The students first outline the arch—going from one end of the paper to the other. They then fill in their band of color. If they want, in addition to just coloring in the band, students can personalize their band by using their name, answers from their Favorite Things Worksheet, and any other cultural symbols they choose.

6. When the students are finished, have them hang their rainbow around the room and give them a chance to look around at the others.

32 Quilts of Many Colors

*K*notted with love the quilts sing on.

—Teresa Palma Acosta

*W*hat my mother teaches me are the essential lessons of the quilt: That people and actions do more in multiple directions at once.

—Elsa Barkley Brown

Background

Quilt making was introduced in America by the early settlers from England and Europe. Patchwork patterns were passed down from generation to generation. Through this handiwork, scraps of fabric were transformed into beautiful and functional bed covers.

The idea of a quilt serves as a good metaphor for appreciating cultural diversity. Made up of many different pieces, with many different colors and shapes, a quilt is held together by a common thread that links all the separate units into a larger whole.

Purpose

Similar to Activity 31, "Colors of the Rainbow," this activity will help students experience the benefits of accepting all people as being interconnected.

Materials

one copy of Quilts Worksheet I or II for each student or a square piece of art paper for each student

magazines (possibly foreign language and travel magazines)

scissors

glue

masking tape

Procedure

1. Discuss the idea of quilts with your students and show them examples. *Kids Making Quilts for Kids* by ABC Quilts (Gualala, CA: Quilt Digest Press, 1992), is an excellent reference book, particularly if you want to make an actual quilt out of fabric.

2. Present the analogy of a quilt as a good way to think about the different peoples of the world who make up all of humanity.

3. Distribute the art materials to the students in their Multicultural Support Teams so that they can share supplies.

4. Instruct the students to cut out pictures from the magazines that relate to them and their culture. For example:

   - Foods they like or traditional foods of their culture
   - Clothes they like or traditional clothes of their culture
   - Products they like or products made in their country of origin
   - Places they have been, would like to visit, or located in their homeland
   - People they admire or with whom they share an ethnic background
   - Words that mean something to them, that express their beliefs and feelings
   - Images of what success and happiness mean to them

5. Ask them to paste the magazine clippings within the pattern on the worksheet to create a design.

6. When the students are finished, have them share their panels with their teammates, explaining what the pictures mean.

7. Next, have the Support Teams tape their panels together to create a quilt of six panels.

8. Now, attach the Support Team quilts together to make one large quilt of the entire class.

9. Find a place in the school where the quilt can be displayed.

10. Conduct a Circle of Friends session to allow the students to talk about their experience of doing the quilt. Discussion topics might include:

    - What I liked about doing the quilt
    - Similarities and differences between my panel and those of other students
    - How I felt when it was all together

    This is a good opportunity to reinforce the idea of the quilt being a metaphor for cultural diversity.

11. You may want to read with your students *The Quilt* by Ann Jonas (New York: Greenwillow, 1984).

Note: Another excellent reference is Quilt Making: A Traditional Woman's Art Form *by Mary Ruthsdotter. Suitable for grades 1 through 6, the set includes complete instructions for an art project with a dozen traditional quilt blocks developed by European immigrants. These and other multicultural materials are available from the National Women's History Project, 7738 Bell Road, Windsor, CA 95492.*

Quilts Worksheet I

Note: *You may want to use a duplicating machine to enlarge this as much as possible before making copies to distribute to students. Heavy art paper is recommended.*

Quilts Worksheet II

33 Honoring Our Ancestors: More Play TV

*My history is bound up in their history
and the generations that follow should know where
they came from to know better who they are.*

—Minnie Miller

Purpose

The aim of this activity is for the students to deepen their appreciation of the lessons they learned in Part II of this book by having them design an entertaining way of communicating one or more of the key points to others through the use of a video recording.

Procedure

As with the video activity at the end of Part I, you have the choice of using the structured activity outlined here or using a creative approach that involves students in designing their own activity.

Structured Approach

1. Tell the students that they are going to create the next episode of their TV show. This time it will be a news program or docudrama that will seek to simulate or re-create events in the lives of our ancestors.

2. In order to stimulate creative thinking, read a story to your students such as *When Justice Failed: The Fred Korematsu Story* by Steven A. Chin (Austin, TX: Steck-Vaughn, 1993), which tells the story of an Asian American who fought the internment order during World War II by which his family—along with the entire West Coast Japanese population—was incarcerated in desolate inland camps. You could also use portions of a video to present aspects of our ancestors' life experiences. Alex Haley's *Roots* is a good example.

3. Next, have the students get their completed worksheet, Highlights of My Ancestors (Activity 20), and bring this with them to their Multicultural Support Team.

4. Each team is to review the stories available on the worksheets and select one that they can re-enact in a five-minute skit or role-play. Encourage them to be creative in thinking about what will make their

skit entertaining: scenery, props, costumes, lighting, dialogue, and so forth.

Give the students a few days to work on collecting or making the items they need for their segment of the TV program.

5. Discuss with the entire group any ideas they have for how to hold the program together: a title or theme, theme music in between the segments, an announcer or host, and so forth.

6. Schedule the day, time, and location for the dress rehearsal and video taping.

7. After the dress rehearsal (which is also video taped), review the tape with the students to discuss what to keep as is and what to change in order to make it even better.

8. Do the final taping, watch the show, and celebrate its success.

9. End with a discussion that might include the following questions:

> "How do you feel about the final program?"
>
> "What did you like about the process of doing this?"
>
> "What did you learn about yourself, each other and our ancestors during the process?"
>
> "Who else would you like to have see the video?"

Creative Approach

1. Let students know that we have come to the end of the second part of this program, and that they will once again have a chance to use the video equipment to make another TV program.

2. Hand out the Key Learning's Part II Worksheet and discuss the points that were covered in these two chapters. Have the students vote on the one or more ideas they would like to use in this activity.

3. Review the list of types of television programs from Activity 17 and, with your students, decide what format to use in order to present the Key Learnings.

4. Give them time to work on the concept, write the script, make the props, rehearse, and so forth.

5. Continue with steps 5 through 9 of the structured approach.

Part II—Key Learnings

Everyone is unique.

All cultures are special.

Everyone belongs here.

I know how to make and keep good friends.

We are all part of a family.

What makes a good friend is the same in all cultures.

Families, like people, are unique.

I am friends with people from all cultures.

My family's family is part of me.

Having friends from different cultures makes my life more interesting.

Part II—Teacher Checklist: Getting to Know My Students and Their Families

❑ Have I taken the time to get to know my students as individuals—their likes and dislikes, fears and dreams?

❑ Have I identified each student's strengths and given each of them opportunities to experience being successful?

❑ Am I helping my students to develop healthy relationships with their classmates, supporting them in solving their own problems, and encouraging them to appreciate cultural diversity?

❑ How well do I know my students' families, and have my efforts to reach out to them been effective?

❑ Have I found ways of facilitating communication with families whose native language is different from mine?

❑ Have I informed my students' parents and guardians about our educational objectives and how they can help at home?

❑ How many families and community members representing all cultures have been in my classroom to interact with the students?

❑ Have I discovered that prejudice among students often reflects biases that they learn from their parents, and have I formulated a plan for educating parents on the value of diversity?

❑ Have I recognized approaches to parenting that do not enhance children's self-esteem, and have I formulated a plan for educating parents on the importance of self-esteem and how it is developed?

Chapter 4—Suggested Student Readings

ABC Quilts. *Kids Making Quilts for Kids.* Gualala, CA: Quilt Digest Press, 1992.

Adler, C. S. *Always and Forever Friends.* New York: Ticknor and Fields, 1988.

Adoff, Arnold. *All the Colors of the Race.* New York: Lothrop, 1982.

Adorjan, Carol. *That's What Friends Are For.* New York: Scholastic, 1990.

Bang, Molly. *The Paper Crane.* New York: Greenwillow, 1985.

Belpré Pura. *The Rainbow-Colored Horse.* New York: Frederick Warner, 1978.

Chin, Steven A. *When Justice Failed: The Fred Korematsu Story.* Austin, TX: Steck-Vaughn, 1993.

Dr. Seuss. *Horton Hears a Who.* New York: Random House, 1954.

Isadora, Rachel. *Friends.* New York: Greenwillow, 1990.

Jakata Stories. *The Value of Friends.* Oakland, CA: Dharma Press, 1990.

Johnson, Tony. *The Quilt Story.* New York: G. P. Putman's Sons, 1985.

Jonas, Ann. *The Quilt.* New York: Greenwillow, 1984.

Peretz, I. L. *The Seven Good Years.* Philadelphia: Jewish Publication Society of America, 1984.

Taylor, Mildred D. *Let the Circle Be Unbroken.* New York: Dial, 1981.

Zolotow, Charlotte. *The Storm Book.* New York: HarperCollins, 1989.

Self-Esteem and Personal Responsibility

Making Life Work

*L*ife is what we make it,
always has been,
always will be.
—Grandma Moses

	Experience (Internal)	Express (External)
Others	Interdependence	Social Responsibility
Self	Independence	Personal Responsibility

Chapter 5

Empowerment

The Force Be with You

The process of empowerment cannot be simplistically defined in accordance with our own particular class interests. We must learn to lift as we climb.
—Angela Davis

Introduction

Mama exhorted her children at every opportunity to "jump at de sun." We might not land on the sun, but at least we would get off the ground.
—Zora Neale Hurston

One day Ying-ying's wish came true. It was a secret wish. She was told that if she asked for her wish then it would not be a secret and wouldn't come true.

It all happened during the Moon Festival of the year she turned seven.

Ying-ying thought it was too hot to wear the clothes her mother made for her to wear during the festival. She wished that she didn't have to share her moon cake rabbit with her cousins and she didn't like having nothing to do while she waited for everyone else to get ready.

She did like her shadow. It followed her everywhere except into the shade. She also liked the unsteady feeling of swaying while on the boat that looked like a floating tea house. The feast with enough moon cake for everyone was more than she could have wished.

Ying-ying didn't want to nap. So, when she was sure that everyone else was asleep, she continued her adventure.

She also didn't really mean to fall into the water. She lost her balance when the firecrackers exploded. Picked up by fishermen, she was left on the shore where she got to see The Moon Lady.

The Moon Lady was singing a sad song about being lost on the moon because of her selfish wishes. Ying-ying cried with her for she too was lost.

After the song, The Moon Lady was supposed to grant everyone one secret wish. Ying-ying had a wish, but before she could say it, she learned the truth about The Moon Lady and the truth about wishes.

"Because I now know there were many kinds of wishes, some that came from my stomach, some that were selfish, some that came from my heart. And I knew what the best wishes were: those I could make come true by myself."*

Students will learn that they too have the power to make their wishes come true. The activities in this chapter are meant to empower students to be responsible for their own experience of self-worth, so that they are able to maintain their self-esteem even in the face of obstacles such as racial prejudice and stereotyping.

Teachers can promote empowerment and critical thinking skills only if they themselves are empowered and critical.

—Jim Cummins

34 Life Purpose Fantasy

Great minds have purposes, others have wishes.
—Washington Irving

Nothing contributes so much to tranquilize the mind as a steady purpose—a point on which the soul may fix its intellectual eye.
—Mary Shelley

Purpose

Just as activities need a purpose to give them meaning, so too people must have a purpose. Without purpose, life becomes pointless, repetitive, and dull.

*The Moon Lady by Amy Tan, illustrated by Gretchen Schields (New York: Macmillan, 1992).

But even though having a purpose is so important to people's happiness, surprisingly few people make the effort to consciously think through and formulate a statement of purpose for their lives. In this process, your students will have a chance to do just that.

The Life Purpose Fantasy provides the answer to a central question when dealing with potential and inner validation. Before doing this activity, conduct a discussion of what the term *life purpose* means. You may want to brainstorm what this concept means to your students. The usual presession comments are very career-related and quite different from the postsession comments.

Materials

drawing paper
colored markers or crayons

Procedure

1. Ask students to get into a comfortable position with their spines straight, either sitting up or lying down. Then ask them to close their eyes and become relaxed, being aware of their breathing. Ask them to take a few deep breaths.

2. Begin the fantasy using the following script:

> *Imagine yourself walking down a road toward a beach.*
>
> *As you approach the beach area, you feel the sun on your face and your arms.*
>
> *Notice the colors and hear the various sounds that are there.*
>
> *Can you hear the ocean as you get closer?*
>
> *As you step onto the sand, you may want to take your shoes off and feel the sand under your feet and between your toes.*
>
> *Does the sand feel warm or cool?*
>
> *As you look around, you find a place on the beach where you can sit down and be alone for awhile.*
>
> *Perhaps you pick a place near where the sand meets the ocean so that you can watch the waves come rolling in.*
>
> *As you watch the waves, you observe the ebb and flow of the tides—the constant movement of the water.*

(For a shortened version, skip to *.)

As you are sitting there on the beach, you notice a large seashell nearby—the kind that you can hold up to your ear and hear the sound of the ocean.

This is a special seashell. It has a special message for you—a message related to your purpose in life.

As you pick up this shell and hold it to your ear, you begin to hear something—a sound, a word, a phrase, a message that reveals something to you about your purpose in life—what your life is all about, the meaning of your existence, your reason for being on earth.

Listen . . .

And now you find yourself nodding your head, but only after you hear this special message and remember it. (Long pause.) Very good!

And now, as you put the shell down and relax, you begin to watch the waves again.

As you do, you notice that coming in on one of the waves there appears to be an old bottle.

Yes, you see that it is a bottle and it looks as if there is a piece of paper or something in it.

As you continue to watch it, the bottle is washed up onto the shore by the waves.

As it rolls up near you, you reach down and pick it up.

As you hold the bottle in your hand, you can feel that it has been worn smooth by the years at sea.

As you look into the bottle, you can see that it contains a message—and the message is for you.

You realize that once again, it is related to your purpose in life—your special mission here on earth.

And so you take the message out of the bottle and read it. Notice what it says and what it means to you . . . (Pause.)

As you commit this message to memory, you put the bottle down and as you do you find your eye is attracted to a stick in the sand.

There seems to be something unusual about this stick, almost as if it were a magical stick.

As you pick up the stick, you notice that it wants to write something in the sand.

As you point the end of the stick, you feel it moving on its own—writing some kind of message in the sand.

As you let the stick move freely, you see that it spells out another message for you about your purpose in life.

When the stick is finished, you stand back and read what the stick has written. (Pause.)

And you realize that each message you have received has given you more and more clarity about your life purpose.

As you think more deeply about this message, you find a place where you can sit down and be comfortable again.

As you relax for a moment, you reflect on the three messages you have received so far and what they mean to you. (Long pause.)

*As you look up, you notice a very wise-looking person walking down the beach.

You have the feeling you know this person.

You recognize this person to be your special guide—someone who knows you and loves you very deeply.

As you invite this guide to sit down with you, you notice how safe and peaceful you feel in this person's presence.

Since this person is very wise and has been sent as your special guide, you have an opportunity to ask this person any questions that you have about your purpose in life and anything else you want to know.

And so you ask your guide, "What is my life purpose?" As the guide begins to speak, you simply listen to your guide's response. (Long pause.)

If you have any other questions, go ahead and talk with your guide and listen carefully to the wisdom being shared with you at this time. (Long pause.)

Very good. Your guide tells you that it is time to leave now, but that you can get in contact any time you want to simply by closing your eyes and coming to this beach.

Any time you feel the need for guidance, your guide will be there ready to help you.

So for now say thank you and good-bye, and get ready to leave the beach.

Moving slowly, stand up, brush off the sand from your clothes, and start walking to the school.

If you've taken your shoes off, take a minute to put them back on now and then continue your walk to the school.

As you enter the school, walk down the hall until you come to our classroom.

Visualize yourself walking back into this room. . . .

Remember what the room looks like. . . .

Remember where you are in the room and who else is here. . . .

Come back now into this room totally and allow yourself to feel good about being here.

When you know you are back here fully and feel good about being here, open your eyes.

3. Ask the students to draw and write about their experience for five minutes.

4. Ask them to get into their Support Teams and share the experience with their group. Give each student three to five minutes to share.

5. You may want to finish with a full-group discussion.

35 Ain't It Awful

The things which hurt, instruct.

—Benjamin Franklin

Character cannot be developed in ease and quiet. Only through experience of trial and suffering can the soul be strengthened, vision cleared, ambition inspired, and success achieved.

—Helen Keller

Purpose

The purpose of this activity is to empower students by encouraging them to be responsible for how they experience situations in life. The activities in this chapter work most effectively as a complete unit, with each exercise following in sequence as they appear.

Procedure

1. Introduce the activity by making remarks similar to these:

"Have you ever thought that it's really crummy being a kid? That adults get to do all the good stuff, while they order kids around and make them do things they themselves don't want to do?"

"Have you ever wished you had a magic button you could push to go directly to age 18 or 21 without all the hassles of growing up?"

"Have you ever had the feeling that adults just don't understand what kids have to put up with these days?"

"If so, you're going to have the chance now to get all your complaints off your chest, once and for all. If you feel that your gripes haven't been heard up to now, today's your day!"

2. Have the students put their chairs into a semicircle. Brainstorm with your class the question "What's so awful about being a kid?" Write the list on the chalkboard.

3. After the brainstorm, read them the story *Alexander and the Terrible, Horrible, No Good, Very Bad Day* by Judith Viorst (New York: Atheneum, 1972).

4. Review with your students the list of "awful things" the class brainstormed, and have them copy the ones they think are the worst, somewhere between five and ten items from the list.

5. Then have them pick out the very worst things about being a kid, from their viewpoint, and draw a picture or write a story about their own terrible, horrible, no good, very bad days.

6. Proceed to Activity 36, "Maybe Yes, Maybe No."

---

36 Maybe Yes, Maybe No

*P*rovidence has hidden a charm in difficult
undertakings which is appreciated only by those
who dare to grapple with them.
                                        —Anne-Sophie Swetchine

*N*othing is good or bad, but thinking makes it so.
                                        —William Shakespeare, *Hamlet*

Purpose

The meaning of life's events lies in our perception or interpretation of them. You may have noticed that different people often have very different interpretations of the same event.

Have you also realized that you sometimes change your own mind about an event after you get more information?

Through this activity, students get to see that there is power in accepting things as they are, in deferring judgment about whether something is good or bad until we see how things turn out.

Procedure

1. Read the following old Chinese Taoist story of "The Man and the Horse" to your class.

   > *A very old Chinese Taoist story describes a farmer in a poor country village. He was considered very well-to-do because he owned a horse which he used for plowing and for transportation. One day his horse ran away. All his neighbors exclaimed how terrible this was, but the farmer simply said, "Maybe yes, maybe no."*
   >
   > *A few days later the horse returned and brought two wild horses with it. The neighbors all rejoiced at his good fortune, but the farmer just said, "Maybe yes, maybe no."*
   >
   > *The next day the farmer's son tried to ride one of the wild horses; the horse threw him and broke his leg. The neighbors all offered their sympathy for his misfortune, but the farmer again said, "Maybe yes, maybe no."*
   >
   > *The next week conscription officers came to the village to take young men for the army. They rejected the farmer's son because of his broken leg. When the neighbors told him how lucky he was the farmer replied, "Maybe yes, maybe no."*

2. Refer back to the list of awful things about being a kid that students wrote for the previous activity. Ask them to consider the possibility that the "awful" events could be looked at from a different viewpoint that would make them appear to be blessings in disguise.

3. Have them select one event from the list and write a brief paragraph explaining what happened, why they thought it was awful, and how they could "reframe" the event to see it as a lucky thing.

4. Next, invite them to look back at the picture they drew of the worst thing about being a kid.

5. Have them pretend that they are looking back on it from several months or years into the future, when enough other things have happened so that they can appreciate how that "worst thing" was actually a necessary step in their lives. Ask them to write a paragraph or two explaining how the "worst thing" they are dealing with today brought them some good luck, taught them a valuable lesson, or turned out not to be so bad after all. (For example, one girl had felt that the worst thing for her was that her best friend was moving away to

another town. She then saw this as an opportunity to become more outgoing so that she could make new friends.)

6. Divide the class into small groups to discuss their stories.

7. Bring the class together again as a full group, and complete the activity with a discussion. Here are some possible discussion questions:

> "Did your reinterpretation of the 'worst thing' agree with those suggested by other members of your group?"

> "Are you beginning to see the situation as not so bad as you first thought? If yes, explain what you now believe to be true about your 'most awful thing.' If no, what would have to happen in order for you to see this situation as less awful?"

> "Consider the situations identified by others as the most awful things about their lives right now. Did they seem that awful to you? Why or why not?"

> "Is it easier to reframe someone else's event than your own?"

> "Does it help to know that other people also have 'worst things' in their lives? Give examples from today's activity to explain your answers."

37 E + R = O

*E*xperience is not what happens to a man;
it is what a man does with what happens to him.
—Aldous Huxley

Purpose

The next three activities work together to demonstrate the concept that we are responsible for our own feelings, to introduce the idea that other people don't "make us" feel things, and to demonstrate that we have control over how we feel and how we react to others.* They are most effective when done as a unit because the students are not asked to interact with the concepts until after the third part, and such interaction is essential to integrating the information into meaningful lessons.

---

*The next three activities are adapted with permission from Jack Canfield. They appear in *101 Ways to Develop Student Self-Esteem and Responsibility: Volume I* by Jack Canfield and Frank Siccone (Boston: Allyn and Bacon, 1993).

People often fall into the trap of blaming other people for how they feel and for what happens to them. Then they end up looking for solutions to their problems by focusing on changing supposed outside causes. It is much more effective to look inside ourselves; regardless of who is to blame, we are at least in charge of how we feel. Taking the point of view that we are responsible for our responses to the outside events gives us more power.

Procedure

1. Write the formula E + R = O on the chalkboard. Then explain the following to the students:

   "**E** stands for all the 'events' of our lives.
   "**R** stands for our 'response' to those events.
   "**O** stands for the 'outcomes' we experience."

2. Continue with the following remarks, seeking ways to involve students and eliciting their comments so that it is more an interactive dialogue than a lecture.

   What most people complain about in their lives are the "outcomes" of this equation. For instance, people complain about feeling hurt, feeling sad, feeling guilty, feeling angry, being yelled at by their parents, being lonely, getting failing grades in school, or how their friends treat them.

   These are all "O's" that resulted from the responses ("R's") used to deal with the events—the "E's"—that occurred.

   For instance, would it be possible to come into this classroom where there are many, many people and end up feeling lonely? ("Yes.") Would it be possible to come into this same classroom and end up making a lot of friends? ("Yes.") It's the same classroom. The "E" is the same: There are the same people, in the same circumstances. Yet two people can enter the same room and produce two very different outcomes for themselves. How is this possible?

   It happens because the "R," the response, of the different individuals is different. For example, I might enter, look around the room, and decide that everyone is too strange, too weird, too unfamiliar, unfriendly, better than I am, or different from me. I would then keep my distance and avoid contact with anyone. The outcome for me would be feeling lonely, thinking that the class was unfriendly, and ending up not having any fun.

   Another person might come into the same room, at the same time, with the same circumstances, and go up to someone and say, "Hi, my name is Sheila, and I just moved here from Cleveland. Who are you?" That person chose a different response to the same set of circumstances and events, the same "E," and as a result, she produced a different outcome in her life.

Often what we do in life is to hope, pray, or demand that the "E," the outside event, change. We often hear this in the form of "If only's." "If only my teacher were more understanding." "If only my father were more loving." "If only my friend understood how I feel." "If only . . ."

The fact is that the "E's"—those environmental influences and the other people in our lives—rarely do change in the way we want them to. It's not impossible, but it doesn't happen very often. In order to produce a different, more desirable outcome, we have to change our own behavior and our own responses.

If I want a different outcome in the classroom, I'm going to have to do something different: reach out, participate more, raise my hand, do my homework on time, or ask for more help from the teacher. If I want a different response from my mother, I'm going to have to do something different in order to get her to respond differently to me.

3. Next, draw the numbers 2 + 2 = 4 on the board.

Now, 2 + 2 = 4 and will always equal 4 from now until the end of time. If you don't like the outcome "4," you will have to change either the first or the second 2. You've already seen that other people and outside events are not likely to change very quickly or easily. But you do have the power to change your response. You can change your 2 to a 3 or 4 or 5 or 6, producing a different result or outcome.

Sometimes the events in your life have already happened. Your friend Shawna's family is going to move out of town. At that point you have a choice—you can choose to be sad by telling yourself that no one will ever like you again the same way Shawna did. You can tell yourself that you're going to be all alone, and then you'll feel lonely. A different response would be to say to yourself, "There are many people in the world with whom I can have a great friendship. I'll start to play with other kids and make new friends right away." This response produces a totally different outcome.

If you hit a baseball through a neighbor's window and start to imagine negative outcomes such as being grounded for a month, you're likely to feel nervous inside—that is the outcome you have produced by imagining a negative event in the future that hasn't happened yet. The baseball going through the window didn't produce that. Your thinking bad thoughts produced it. Another choice is to realize that you've made a mistake. You can own up to it, talk to the neighbor, and work to replace the window. Then you'll produce a good feeling inside of yourself. The event does not determine how you feel. What you say to yourself (auditory) and what pictures you choose to run in your head (visual) determine how you feel.

"E + R = O" means that if you want changes in your life, you need to stop blaming the events, circumstances, and other people for

what happens to you and start focusing on your thoughts, internal images, and actions—your response. That's where your power is to produce the kinds of outcomes you truly want.

38 Green Hair

*S*ome things have to be believed to be seen.
—Ralph Hodgson

Purpose

This interactive demonstration helps make the explanation about "E + R = O" even more real for students.

Procedure

1. Say the following:

   The "E + R = O" formula works well in terms of seeing how we let other people make us feel bad. For example, suppose I go up to Mary and tell her, "Mary, you have green hair." Would that make you feel bad? (Mary would usually answer no. If she says yes, keep asking different students until someone says no.) "Why not?" "Because I know I don't have green hair." So it's not what I say to Mary that affects how she feels. What Mary believes to be true about her hair is what determines her emotional response to me.

   Any time someone says something to you and you feel hurt, that's because at some level you have a doubt about yourself in that area. If I say, "You have green hair!" and you know you don't, there is no problem. The same is true with anything else in your life. If someone calls you stupid and you feel hurt by it, they didn't hurt your feelings. Your self-doubt about your own intelligence is what created the pain. (The way to get beyond this is to use affirmations, such as "I am an intelligent person. I am smart.")

2. At this point, conduct a discussion about things people have said that have hurt your students. Ask them to look inside to see if they have self-doubts about that particular issue in their lives.

   By now, your classroom environment should be safe enough for students to feel comfortable talking about racial slurs and how they respond to such name calling. You might ask, "What names have you been called that have negative connotations (for example, wop, kike, nigger, fag or faggot)? Does anyone know the origins of these terms? What are they supposed to mean? What is hurtful or offensive to you about these words? How can we hear them without taking it personally or without being hurt or offended?"

3. Point out that much of our self-image—including our self-doubts and hurts—is a function of early environmental factors such as parent and family admonitions, cultural and societal prejudices, and so forth. By taking responsibility for ourselves, we have the opportunity to get out from under these influences.

4. Second, even though we now realize that each of us can experience being responsible for our own self-doubts and hurts, this does not give us permission to be insensitive and cruel to others, as in putting down and teasing others.

Note: It is important that you as the adult role model be comfortable discussing these terms with your students. It might help to check out the origins of these terms and how they came into common usage.

wop   *According to one story, when Italian immigrants arrived in the United States, they were instructed to <u>W</u>ait <u>O</u>n <u>P</u>ier. Apparently these letters, posted on signs above where the people were standing, became linked to them as a derogatory nickname.*

faggot   *One source explains that in the days of Joan of Arc, when people were burned at the stake, homosexuals were deemed of such little value that they were used as firewood to keep the flames burning. Fagot is, in fact, a term for a bundle of twigs, sticks, or branches bound together especially for firewood.*

You may want to discuss these racial slurs with a colleague to be sure you will be comfortable in using these terms with your students.

Another strategy for neutralizing any emotional charge that certain words have is to repeat the word out loud over and over again until it begins to sound like gibberish. You can do this with your students if they seem to be particularly affected by any of the terms.

39 The Biggest Idiot

Purpose

This demonstration simply takes the concept of insults and hurtful remarks a bit further. When students assimilate this example, they will have taken a big step toward taking full responsibility for their internal experiences.

Procedure

1. Continue the discussion.

   Suppose I approach John and say, "John, of all the people I've ever met in my ten years of teaching, you have to be the biggest idiot I have ever had in one of my classes." How many of you would think it would raise John's self-esteem if I said that to John? (No students raise their hands.) How many of you think that statement would lower John's self-esteem? (Most students raise their hands.)

   How many of you think it doesn't matter what I say to John but, rather, what John says to himself after I stop talking that affects his self-esteem? (Students who have been paying attention will raise their hands.)

   It's important that you understand fully that it's not what I say to John, but what John says to John after I stop talking that affects how he feels about himself.

   If John reacts by saying to himself, "My gosh, how did he find out so soon?" that will affect his self-esteem in a negative way. But if he responds by saying to himself, "Well, the teacher just picked on me because he knows that I have a strong self-concept and can take this kind of kidding," John will feel good about himself.

   Remember, when someone says something to you that hurts, look inside and see what you are telling yourself about yourself.

2. To complete this discussion, answer students' questions. Then challenge them to hold the attitude—at least in this class—that nobody else *makes* them feel anything, and that they don't *make* other people feel good or bad either. We have to take greater responsibility for how we make ourselves feel by what we tell ourselves about what other people say.

3. At this point, return to the idea of E + R = O. Have students move into small groups and brainstorm at least six things they can say to them-

selves (R) when someone calls them a name or tries to put them down (E), so that they will be able to maintain their self-respect (O).

Possible internal statement (R):

"No matter what you say, I'm still O.K."

"I am somebody special."

"I am proud of my cultural heritage."

"What you're saying has nothing to do with me."

"Too bad that you can't see me for who I really am."

"If they had any real experience at all they would know that the stereotype is not true."

"I know I'm smart. They must not be paying attention."

4. End the lesson by having each small group report back to the entire class the statements they created.

Note: This series of activities takes an extreme position in order to make the point that external events only cause us to feel or act in certain ways to the extent to which we allow them to have that kind of power over us.

This is an insight that is meant to empower students through the realization that even when they cannot *control the* events *of their lives, they* can *determine how they* respond *to these circumstances.*

This potential that human beings have for transcending their circumstances must be underscored if cycles of poverty, violence, bigotry, drug addiction, and so forth are ever to be broken.

At the same time, we should not lose sight of the dynamic interrelationship between self and others, as discussed in the introduction to this book. That a person's self-image is constructed in a social context is precisely why this book has been given a multicultural perspective.

Perhaps it would help to distinguish between functional *and* dysfunctional *influences.*

I once had the opportunity to counsel a third-grader who was constantly in trouble. My attempts to get at the root causes of the problem resulted in a series of typical responses:

"I didn't do it. The other kid did and I got blamed."

"The teacher doesn't like me."

"I don't know."

After a few exchanges, the child said, "Maybe I'm just a bad boy." When I asked him where he got that idea, he said, "My kindergarten teacher told me I was a bad boy." Apparently he believed her and has been behaving consistent with that self-image ever since.

This is an example of dysfunctional influence. If the child had the concept $E + R = O$, he might have been able to hear his teacher's comment as an expression of her displeasure with his behavior *rather than as a condemnation of his* being.

That he did not have this awareness or the maturity to apply it should not be blamed on him. No one who feels helpless and victimized by circumstances should be blamed for this.

If, however, helping to create an awareness of the possibility of transcending these circumstances proves to be empowering, then such influence would be deemed functional. Strengthening my own ability to validate those influences that are life-enhancing and discard those that are not is the ultimate in functionality—and, with respect to the point of this activity, the ultimate in personal responsibility/response-ability (i.e., the ability to respond).

I am still determined to be cheerful and happy in whatever situation I may be, for I have also learned from experience that the greater part of our happiness or misery depends on our dispositions and not on our circumstances.

—Martha Washington

40 Dear Abby: The Nose Better Letter

It is almost impossible to throw dirt on someone without getting a little on yourself.

—Abigail Van Buren

Purpose

Responsibility means recognizing yourself as the cause of your responses to things that happen in your life. When you are being responsible, you are aware that you are the source of your thoughts, feelings, and behavior.

In this activity, students look at an example of a person who doesn't know that he or she is responsible for him- or herself, and see how that person could take more responsibility for his or her life. They then get an opportunity to deal with an area of their lives where they themselves could become more powerful.

Procedure

1. Have your students read the letter to Dear Abby on the Dear Abby Worksheet provided. (This could also be read aloud to the class by you or one of the students.)

2. Ask them to read and think about the questions on the second page of the worksheet.

3. Now have them write a reply to Nose Better on the third page of the worksheet as though they were Dear Abby.

4. Have them form groups of five students each. They are to take turns reading the Dear Abby replies they wrote. Suggest that they look for similarities and differences in the advice each of them gave to Nose Better.

5. Next, ask students to write their own letters to Dear Abby on the fourth page of the worksheet, complaining to her about the problems they identified as the worst thing about being themselves or any other problem they are dealing with at the moment. Invite them to see if they can outdo Nose Better by blaming other people, going into detail about how these problems are somebody else's fault. Tell them to lay it on thick!

6. When they have finished writing their letters, suggest that they consider in what way they have been looking at their own problems irresponsibly—as though they were not the source of their own feelings, thoughts, and behavior but as though someone else had power or control over their responses. "Have you been acting like Nose Better, who was blaming her unhappiness on the doctor rather than looking at what she could do to make friends?"

7. Now ask them to pretend that they are Abby. Have them write Abby's reply to their own letters. Instruct them to make sure that Abby lets them know how they were being irresponsible in their attitude toward the problem.

8. Ask the students to get back into their groups and take turns reading their letters and replies aloud. Suggest that they ask the other people in their group for any feedback they have about the problems and Abby's advice.

9. Bring the full class together to discuss the activity. Discussion questions might include the following:

> "How did it feel being an advice columnist? Do you have a new career goal?"
>
> "Did you discover that you had some good advice to give yourself? Did it turn out that you already knew some things to do about your problem?"
>
> "Which Dear Abby answer was easier for you to write, the one to Nose Better or the one to yourself? How can you explain this?"

Dear Abby Worksheet

Read the following letter.

Dear Abby,

My problem is my nose. It was too big and made me feel ugly so I had plastic surgery. The doctor botched the job, and so I had it done by another surgeon. Now it is even worse.

My nose now comes up in a point and makes me look stuck up. That's why I don't have any friends, and I'm so unhappy.

Don't advise me to see a psychiatrist. I did this and he said it was in my mind. It is not my mind that's the problem, it's my nose.

What should I do?

—Nose Better*

Dear Abby Worksheet (continued)

Questions to consider before writing your response:

1. From Nose Better's point of view, who or what has power over his or her happiness?

   _____

   _____

2. Think about your classmates. How important is the shape of their noses in determining whether you like them? What do you look for when choosing your friends?

   _____

   _____

3. What other things do you think Nose Better might be doing to keep him- or herself from having friends?

   _____

   _____

4. What do you think is the real source of the problem?

   _____

5. What changes do you think Nose Better might be able to make within him- or herself that might help him or her have more friends and be happier?

   _____

   _____

   _____

   _____

Dear Abby Worksheet (continued)

Dear Nose Better,

_____

_____

_____

_____

_____

_____

_____

_____

_____

_____

_____

_____

Sincerely,

Abby

Dear Abby Worksheet (continued)

My letter to Dear Abby:

Dear Abby,

_____

_____

_____

_____

_____

_____

_____

Signed,

_____

Dear Abby's response to my letter:

Dear _____,

_____

_____

_____

_____

_____

_____

_____

Sincerely,

Abby

41   Shattering Stereotypes*

Every bigot was once a child free of prejudice.
—Sister Mary De Lourdes

Purpose

To help students recognize and analyze the myths of stereotyping, become aware of forces that influence stereotyping, and learn to relate to people free from the limits of stereotypes.

Materials

Fact Sheets A-B-C
pencils

Procedure

1. In a large group, explain the purpose of the activity and use Fact Sheets to introduce the topic of stereotypes (copy or use as a transparency).

2. Divide the class into small discussion groups (six to eight members). Their support groups can be used for this purpose.

3. Distribute the Shattering Stereotypes Worksheet. Have the students complete them and then share their individual responses with their small group.

4. Reassemble as a large group and discuss:

   "What do you think stereotyping is?"

   "What were the stereotypes discussed in your group?"

   "Which stereotypes bother you the most?"

   "How do we learn stereotypes?"

   "What can we do to eliminate stereotyping?"

   "How can we deal with people who tease us by using ethnic humor or slurs?"

*This and the following activity, "Guess Who?," were adapted with permission from *Pupils' Adjustment in a Desegregated Setting (PADS),* Cleveland Public Schools, 1978. © 1978, 1994, Hanoch McCarty (Ed.). For information about similar activities and training, write P.O. Box 66, Galt, CA 95632.

5. Remind students of the lessons learned in "E + R = O," "Green Hair," and "The Biggest Idiot" (Activities 37, 38, and 39).

You can also teach them the five-step program developed by the Anti-Defamation League's A World of Difference Institute, summarized on the Dealing with Prejudice Worksheet (page 139).

Note: The examples of stereotypes used on Fact Sheet A are taken from a survey conducted in 1994 by Louis Harris on behalf of the National Conference of Christians and Jews.

The poll discovered that not only does bigotry esist among white Americans, but ethnic groups believe stereotypes about each other. For example, a majority of Asians believe Latinos tend to have more children than they can support. Latinos consider blacks are inclined toward crime and violence. African Americans, in turn, believe that Latinos lack the drive to succeed and that Asians are devious in business dealings.

The good news emerging from this study is that younger respondents were less likely than older respondents to hold negative stereotypes of other ethnic groups in every category.

Fact Sheet A

Definition of a stereotype:
to categorize a group based on some presupposed characteristics.

- Stereotypes may be negative and/or positive.
- Stereotypes are learned.

Examples:

- Muslims belong to a religion that condones or supports terrorism.
- Latinos tend to have bigger families than they are able to support.
- African Americans want to live on welfare.
- Jews, when it comes to choosing between people and money, will choose money.
- Asian Americans are unscrupulously crafty and devious in business.
- Whites are insensitive to other people and have a long history of bigotry and prejudice.

Fact Sheet B

What are some stereotyping techniques?

- Exaggeration or distortion of a physical feature or behavior
- Use of key words or phrases (words that overgeneralize)

Examples:

- Use of loaded words (words that may create negative images)

Examples:

slobs	pigs
untrained	dangerous
welfare	poverty

Fact Sheet C
How we learn stereotypes:

- neighbors
- friends
- movies
- school books
- library books
- comic books
- family
- television
- cartoons

Shattering Stereotypes Worksheet

Directions: *Complete each statement with the name of a group which you feel is most commonly stereotyped. Next, put a T or an F in the column to show whether you believe that this statement is True or False. Then, in the last column, write in the name of someone you know or know about who does not fit the stereotype.*

	True or False	Name of Someone Who Does Not Fit the Stereotype
1. Most _____ wear feathers and live in teepees.	____	_____
2. _____ are pretty but dumb.	____	_____
3. Most _____ people are stingy.	____	_____
4. Most _____ have fat wives and lots of children.	____	_____
5. Most _____ families are on welfare	____	_____
6. _____ cannot be trusted.	____	_____
7. _____ all look alike.	____	_____
8. _____ really like to drink.	____	_____
9. _____ usually hang around in street gangs.	____	_____
10. _____ are stronger and smarter than _____.	____	_____
11. _____ have good singing voices and dance well.	____	_____
12. Most _____ own their own businesses.	____	_____
13. _____ are not good at math.	____	_____
14. _____ are rednecks who wear cowboy hats, drink beer, and hate people who are different.	____	_____

Dealing with Prejudice Worksheet*

1. Don't respond by making an equally offensive remark, and don't embarrass the person who made the remark or told the joke.

2. Talk with the person privately to remove his or her need to save face or defend his or her actions.

3. Start the conversation by ``vesting your relationship.'' People listen better when they know they matter to the person who is speaking. Start the conversation by saying something such as: ``I wanted to talk with you, Mary, because our friendship is very important to me.''

4. Use ``I'' statements, not ``you'' statements. The point of this conversation is to let the offender know how ``I'' felt about what was said. It is not intended to be a conversation about what ``you'' did wrong.

5. Remember your rights. You do not have the right to dictate someone else's sense of humor. You do, however, have the right to ask that this type of humor not be used in your presence.

*Used with permission from the Anti-Defamation League, A World of Difference Institute, New York.

42 Guess Who?

*Prejudices, it is well known, are most difficult
to eradicate from the heart whose soil has
never been loosened or fertilized by education;
they grow there, firm as weeds among stones.*

—Charlotte Brontë

Purpose

This activity continues the theme of stereotypes and is designed to demonstrate how prejudgments can be inaccurate. It will help students see the value of deferring judgment about an individual until they have adequate information, and to avoid making assumptions about who people are and what they can achieve on the basis of limited stereotypes.

Materials

paper and pencil

Procedure

1. Read the true but incomplete stories included here.
2. Ask the students to think about how the five children turned out as adults and to write the rest of the story.
3. Have the students share their conclusions.
4. Reveal the true identity of each individual and discuss the following:

   "Were you surprised at the true identity of any person? Why?"

   "What information in the story did you use as a basis for your conclusion?"

   "What qualities do you feel these people might have had that helped them overcome many of the obstacles they faced?"

   "Have you ever judged someone else and later found out you were wrong? How did you feel?"

   "Have you ever been judged unfairly by others? How did you feel?"

   "What information is necessary before you can make an accurate judgment about others?"

5. Now have each student write a one-paragraph autobiography describing his or her life to date, highlighting unique aspects of his or her story, especially those events that others might use to predict future success or failure.

6. Now have each student write his or her own ending to the story describing how things turned out for him or her as adults and what he or she accomplished during his or her lifetime.

7. You can have the students read their own stories, or you could collect them and read the first part of some of the stories aloud, keeping the author anonymous. The rest of the students could write the second half of the story—what they think became of this student as an adult. Then the student whose life it is would identify him- or herself and read what he or she wrote as the adult version.

8. End the activity with a discussion of the importance of believing that everyone has the potential to succeed.

Guess Who?

Story One

The young girl in this story was not allowed to go to grade school. When she did go out in public she was dressed oddly. As she grew older, she felt rejected by both parents. She even resorted to strange acts, such as swallowing large items, to receive the attention she desired. When her parents died, she lived with grandparents. Her grandfather was alcoholic and her grandmother was very strict.

Her childhood played a significant role in her later development. As an adult she . . .

Story Two

A ``spoiled brat'' is perhaps the best way to describe this young boy's moodiness and, at times, unpleasantly agressive behavior. Although he was willing to practice and showed an ability to learn music quickly, there was no evidence that he would ever be much beyond average.

With tolerance and encouragement from his family, however, he . . .

Story Three

The word *strange* seems to fit the early years of this young man. A fever at birth caused him to be born with an overly large head. He was accused of starting numerous fires as a child and as a result was labeled a ``firebug.'' His childhood brought him much frustration.

Throughout his later years . . .

Story Four

This child came close to death many times early in life. From problems associated with his birth, to an early experience with kidnappers, his developing years were tough. He was kept separate from other children by not being allowed to go to school.

This social separation and his poor physical health caused him . . .

Story Five

At one time, this young woman was a drug addict. As a divorced woman with a baby daughter, she took odd jobs, including working as a cosmetician in a funeral parlor, and for four or five years she was on welfare.

She eventually ended up . . .

Guess Who? Answers

Story One

The girl with the strict grandmother, who was not allowed friends and was kept from school was Eleanor Roosevelt. She was to become a great social leader, author, and lecturer, as well as the wife of U.S. President Franklin Roosevelt.

Story Two

The moody child would triumph over his recurring emotional problems to become a towering legend of classical music. Vladimir Horowitz came to be hailed as ''the king of piano virtuosos, the most charismatic performer since Franz Liszt.''

Story Three

The large-headed boy, who the teachers thought was ''mentally ill,'' was Thomas A. Edison. Mr. Edison invented the light bulb, phonograph, and more than a thousand other things that make life better for us all.

Story Four

The baby who was born weak and small, with no hope for the future, grew into one of the great scientists of this country. He helped not only his own people but all the people of the world. He made many great discoveries, including 300 uses for the peanut. This man was George Washington Carver.

Story Five

This welfare mother finally got her break in show business doing a one-woman performance piece that landed her on Broadway. She was nominated for an Oscar for her first movie role in *The Color Purple* and later won the award for *Ghost.* Whoopi Goldberg continues to make movies, has had her own television show, has written a children's book, and is involved in many charitable and advocacy projects, such as Comic Relief, which raises millions of dollars for the nation's homeless.

42 Odd Jobs Scavenger Hunt

Historically our own culture has relied for the creation of rich and contrasting values upon many artificial distinctions, the most striking of which is sex . . . if we are to achieve a richer culture, rich in contrasting values, we must recognize the whole gamut of human possibilities, and so weave a less arbitrary social fabric, one in which each diverse human gift will find a fitting place.
                                                              —Margaret Mead

Background

Gender-based stereotypes also need to be challenged. Since women have entered the work force, some progress has been made in gaining parity with men, but much remains to be done. Women continue to earn less than men, and the number of women in high-level executive positions remains small.

Research indicates a pattern of diminishing self-esteem as girls grow older. "Younger girls tend to be much more confident, reliant and straight-forward, " according to Annie G. Rogers, researcher associate at the Harvard Project on the Psychology of Women and the Development of Girls.

Among the many studies that have documented the phenomenon, a 1990 nationwide poll commissioned by the American Association of University Women revealed a dramatic drop in self-esteem among girls as they enter adolescence.

Using a basic self-esteem indicator to track positive feelings about one-self, the ratings in elementary school revealed that 67 percent of the boys and 60 percent of the girls had high self-regard. By the time the children reached middle school, the numbers had decreased slightly for the boys, to 56 percent, and more sharply for the girls, of whom only 37 percent maintained high self-esteem. By high school, only 29 percent of the girls had high self-esteem.

While many factors may contribute to this decline, schools certainly have an important role to play in building self-confidence and keeping possibilities open for all students. Research has shown that teacher behavior often reinforces the message that boys are more capable and more important than girls. At all grade levels, for example, boys get more attention from teachers and more positive feedback. One recent study showed that young black girls get the least positive attention from teachers.

Clearly, we must be more diligent in how we interact with all children, making sure that they learn from us in every possible way that we believe in them and know that they can succeed.

We make too much of it; we are men and women in the second place, human beings in the first.
—Olive Schreiner

The test for whether or not you can hold a job should not be the arrangement of your chromosomes.
—Bella Abzug

Purpose

The purpose of this activity is to encourage students to move beyond limiting notions of what's possible for them, and to encourage them to visualize themselves being successful in any field of endeavor, regardless of their gender.

Procedure

1. You can introduce this activity by reading *He Bear, She Bear* by Stan and Jan Berenstain (New York: Random House, 1974) or *William's Doll* by Charlotte Zolotow (New York: Harper & Row, 1972). Give students the opportunity to share their thoughts and feelings about the book.

2. Continue the discussion by having the students brainstorm as many jobs or careers as they can. Record these on the board or on butcher paper. You might find it helpful to go through the letters of the alphabet, looking for jobs that begin with each letter.

3. Next, ask the students which of the jobs can be done by both men and women and which ones are only for men or only for women. Record the students' comments by putting a W (women), M (men), or W/M (both) next to each job name.

4. Discuss with your students the jobs that are labeled W/M as being appropriate for both women and men. Find out if they know people who work in these areas and what they think these jobs are like.

   Ask if each of these jobs has always been done by both men and women, or whether there was a time when it was done only by women or only by men.

5. Now tell the students that they are going on a Scavenger Hunt. Be sure they are familiar with the term. If not, explain that a scavenger hunt is a game in which you try to find a number of items within a given time frame or before another team does.

In our scavenger hunt, we will find women who are doing jobs we think are only for men and men who are doing jobs we think are just for women.

Explore with your students how they might go about finding these people. Possibilities include:

- Using a telephone directory
- Asking family members, friends, and other people in the community
- Checking with the librarian to see if he or she could help
- Contacting a professional association that represents the occupation

6. Explain that they will be working in teams to complete this project. Points will be given as follows:

2 points	•	Find the name of a person who works at one of these jobs.
10 points	•	Interview the person by phone or in person to fill out the Scavenger Hunt Interview Form.
20 points	•	Visit the person at his or her job site and report back to the entire class what you learned. Perhaps you could bring in photographs of the person on the job.
30 points	•	Invite the person to come to class and talk about his or her job experience.

Agree on how long to provide for the project (one to three weeks). Find as many people as you can within the time frame. The team with the greatest number of points wins.

7. Have the students get into their support teams or divide them into teams in some other way and give them some time to plan how they are going to work together to win the scavenger hunt.

8. At the end of the agreed-upon time frame, have the students report on their findings.

9. Complete the activity with a discussion of what they have learned about job opportunities and how this relates to their own possible career choices.

The best career advice given to the young is "Find out what you like doing best and get someone to pay you for doing it."
—Katherine Whitehorn

Scavenger Hunt Interview Form

1. What is your name? _____

_____

2. What is your occupation? _____

_____

3. How long have you been doing this kind of work? _____

_____

4. What kind of qualifications or training do you need for this job?

_____

_____

_____

5. How did being a man/woman help or hinder you in getting this job? _____

_____

_____

6. What do you like most about your job? _____

_____

_____

7. What do you like least about your job? _____

_____

_____

8. What advice do you have for young people who might be thinking about this as a career? _____

_____

_____

_____

44 From Victim to Victor

Language is the road map of a culture. It tells you where its people come from and where they are going.
—Rita Mae Brown

Victim status not only confers the moral superiority of innocence. It enables people to avoid taking responsibility for their own behavior.
—John Taylor

Background

The language that we use to describe ourselves and the events in our lives plays a primary role in shaping how we perceive and experience ourselves and our lives.

When the AIDS epidemic hit, people who were infected with the virus were commonly referred to as "victims" of the disease. A further distinction was made by labeling some people as "innocent victims," as if others who had AIDS were "guilty victims."

Since being a victim is the exact opposite of empowerment, it became vitally important to transform the way people talked about the disease. The preferred term became "People Living with AIDS," which allowed for the possibility that not everyone who was infected would die and that, while alive, people with AIDS still maintained their inalienable rights to life, liberty, and the pursuit of happiness.

In many ways, the United States seems to have become a society of victims. Consider the case of Rose Cipollone, who developed lung cancer and blamed the tobacco companies for the fact that she had smoked a pack and a half of cigarettes a day for forty years. What was her responsibility for this?

Or how about the so-called Twinkie defense used by Dan White, who claimed that he was a victim of temporary insanity caused by eating junk food, and thus was not responsible for killing San Francisco Mayor George Moscone and Supervisor Harvey Milk.

A similar insanity defense was used by Nancy Berchtold, who sought to be excused from killing her baby because she said she was suffering from postpartum psychosis.

More and more Americans from all walks of life, all cultures, ages, and incomes seem to be adopting the status of victim: victims of "dysfunctional families," of "codependent relationships," of addictions, of economic indicators, and of teachers' low expectations, government graft, bureaucratic boondoggles, professional malpractice, racism, sexism, ageism, homophobia, and so forth.

This is not to deny that these conditions exist and need to be changed. The trick is to engage in the process of transforming society from a place of power rather than pain, responsibility rather than resentment, and collaboration rather than condemnation.

Purpose

The purpose of this activity is to challenge students to accept responsibility for living in a world that needs hope, healing, and healthy alternatives, and to feel empowered by the opportunities this provides for them to make a real difference.

Procedure

Part One

1. Introduce this activity by making some of the points presented in the Background and Purpose sections. You may want to refer to famous people such as President Clinton, who did not settle for being the victims of difficult childhood situations but, rather, became victorious over their circumstances.

2. Brainstorm with your class all the things they don't like about the state of the world: unemployment, homelessness, poverty, crime, starvation, war, drugs, and so on.

3. Ask the students to think about which of the bad things in the world have had the most impact on them personally; which, if any, they have had to deal with directly at home, at school, in their neighborhood or community.

    Decide on the best way for your students to share their experiences:

    - In a letter to themselves, to you, to their special guide, to someone they want to help, to someone they want to forgive, or to someone they think can do something about the situation
    - In a drawing illustrating the circumstances that concern them
    - In a collage, cutting out pictures and words from magazines that illustrate the conditions they want to change
    - In pairs, sharing with a classmate about the situation and how they feel about it
    - In their support groups

However you structure it, be sure that the students feel safe, have them agree to confidentiality; and remind them that, as always, they are free to pass if they prefer not to share.

4. After the students have had an opportunity to share their experiences in whatever format you have selected, bring them together again as a full group and ask them to share the insights they have gained from the activity thus far.

Part Two

1. Next, tell the students that one way of moving from feeling like a VICTIM of these circumstances to feeling more like a VICTOR is to create a vision of a better world and to dedicate themselves to doing something to bring this positive vision to life.

   Ask the students to write, draw, or talk with their partner or support group about their own vision of a better world.

2. Again, bring the entire class together, and invite those who are willing to share their vision.

Part Three

1. Have the students write, draw, and talk about what they could do to help make their vision of a better world come true.

   For example, if hunger is an area of concern, then the students might consider starting a schoolwide drive to collect canned goods to donate to a local soup kitchen. If crime is a concern, they might vow to be honest and not cheat or steal.

2. Complete the activity by having students return to the class circle and share what they are going to do to make a positive difference and how they feel about it. The process, of course, doesn't end here. Encourage students actually to carry out their plans, and provide future opportunities for them to report back to the class on their accomplishments.

   One approach is to have the class choose one project to work on together. (Refer to Activity 69, "Community Service Projects," for further ideas.)

45   Power Full

*Make the best use of what is in your power,
and take the rest as it happens.*

—Epictetus

Purpose

This activity is designed to support students in experiencing a greater sense of potency and inner strength that they can tap into when they want to achieve a goal.

Procedure

1. Have the students sit around in a circle. Suggest to them that each of us has within ourselves a source of power. Tell them that the purpose of this activity is for them to feel their own inner strength.

2. Ask them to close their eyes and imagine a place in their bodies where they will find their source of power.

    With your eyes closed, connect with the spot within your body from which your inner strength and power will come.

    Maybe you are noticing that it is coming from your heart or the top of your head or the palms of your hands or the bottom of your feet.

    There is no right place for it to be. Wherever it is for you is fine.

    Once you have located your source of power, imagine that it is a source of light, warm, clear, pure light.

    Now, let the light get brighter and grow so that it is expanding to fill more and more of your body. Continue until the light has grown to fill your entire body. When you feel that your entire body is full of light, and full of your personal power, please open your eyes.

3. If some students finish before others, ask them to wait quietly until all students have opened their eyes.

4. Give the students an opportunity to share what the experience was like for them.

5. Next, have the students identify an upcoming event at which they are looking to perform well—play well at a ball game, dance well at a

recital, present themselves well at a speech, do well on a test, and so forth.

6. Now, while they are thinking about their goal, have them close their eyes once again and recreate their source of light expanding to fill their bodies with that power to succeed.

7. Encourage your students to repeat this process each time they intend to succeed at something.

Chapter 5—Suggested Student Readings

Berenstain, Stan, & Jan Berenstain. *He Bear, She Bear*. New York: Random House, 1974.

Larrick, Nancy. *City Streets*. New York: M. Evans, 1968.

Merriam, Eve. *Mommies at Work*. New York: Simon and Schuster, 1989.

Silverstein, Shel. *A Light in the Attic*. New York: Harper & Row, 1981.

Tan, Amy & Gretchen Schields. *The Moon Lady*. New York: Macmillan, 1992.

Uchida, Yoshiko. *The Best Bad Thing*. New York: Atheneum, 1983.

Viorst, Judith. *Alexander and the Terrible, Horrible, No Good, Very Bad Day*. New York: Atheneum, 1972.

Zemach, Margot. *It Could Always Be Worse*. New York: Scholastic, 1976.

Zolotow, Charlotte. *William's Doll*. New York: Harper & Row, 1972.

$$Chapter \quad 6$$

Achievement
Celebrating Success

Accomplishments have no color.
—Leontyne Price

Introduction

*I must admit that I personally measure success
in terms of the contribution an individual makes
to her or his fellow human beings.*

—Margaret Mead

Once upon a time in Medieval Spain lived a woman named Truhana. Each year she would go to market to sell honey—one of the few things of value that this poor woman had.

On the way to market, carrying the jar of honey on her head, she began to fantasize about the money she would make. She would sell the honey and then use the money to buy eggs. The eggs, in turn, would be hatched by her hens, producing plenty of little chickens. The chickens could be sold.

Lambs could be bought. On and on she dreamed.

Great wealth would be hers. She would be richer than her neighbors. Her sons and daughters would marry well, and people would comment on how remarkable it was that such a poverty-stricken woman had become so rich.

Entranced by these pleasurable thoughts, she began preening herself and laughing heartily. Suddenly, the jar of honey fell from her head and smashed upon the ground. Her dreams of great wealth smashed along with it.

Sometimes the very means to real success are lost by dwelling on the fantasy or illusion of success.*

Although a vision of success is essential, paying attention to the steps along the way is crucial. In this section, students will learn to envision themselves as successful, and they will practice skills necessary to actually achieve success. These include setting and tracking goals, and choosing excellence over excuses.

46   Success Is . . .

Success is getting what you want.
Happiness is wanting what you get.

—Anonymous

Background

Why do some students succeed in school, while others fail? Theories abound. What is most intriguing is that there are students who succeed despite all odds. They are able to transcend what for most are debilitating circumstances. What is the secret to their motivation?

It is useful to consider human motivation as an analysis—conscious or not—of the costs versus the benefits of any given endeavor. After we weigh the investment required and the risks involved against the potential benefits, if the benefits outweigh the costs we are motivated to act. If the costs are too great and without sufficient payoff, we will not pursue a particular course of action.

All students must invest to a certain degree in order to achieve success. Attending classes rather than hanging out with friends, studying rather than listening to music, risking giving the wrong answer—these are all costs.

Students who receive encouragement and rewards at home and also imagine long-term rewards in terms of greater career opportunities are likely to think that the benefits are worth the effort. Intrinsically motivated students, for whom the joy of learning and the personal feeling of accomplishment are their own rewards, are also likely to make the investment.

---

*This folktale, perhaps the best known parable in the world, is adapted from "Don't Count Your Chickens" in *World Tales* by Idries Shah (New York: Harcourt Brace Jovanovich, 1979).

Making that effort is more difficult, however, for students whose family and community show little evidence that school success is the road to better jobs and improved quality of life. Add to that a peer culture in which being good in school is seen as selling out, and you've increased the cost and reduced the benefits considerably.

If these costs are compounded by a school experience of being excluded and devalued, then, clearly, the costs will appear too great and the payoffs too small to justify the effort.

Although schools may not be able to influence the job situation in today's economy, they can help eliminate barriers for women and people of color by developing in today's students—the next generation of citizens—a greater appreciation for and celebration of diversity.

In the short term, schools can create learning environments where students—all students—feel included, where the curriculum reflects the struggles and strengths of all peoples, and where all students are esteemed for being who they are.

In this activity, students are asked to define success. You might ask them to consider the costs and benefits of success. What are some of the ways students resist school—misbehavior, vandalism, dropping out, and so forth. What would make the education exchange worth it? How can they maintain their sense of self and sense of cultural identity—and still succeed?

Purpose

For students to explore what is meant by success—how achievement is defined by society, their culture, their family, their peers, and themselves.

Procedure

1. Write the word *success* on the board and ask the students what it means. Write down their responses on butcher paper divided into sections—our class, our friends, our families, our society.

2. Continue to explore the idea of *success* by asking the class how society at large defines success. For example, what images are projected in the media of success? What kinds of people are spotlighted as being successful?

   - Ask the students what their parents and families think of as being successful.
   - Now see what their friends and peers mean by success. Do they have the same values as families and society? Discuss commonalities and variations.
   - How about the students' personal definition of success? How great is the influence of these other groups?

- Discuss the relationship between *success* and *happiness.* How are these the same or different? Can someone be happy yet not successful? Successful but not happy?

3. Have the students move into their Multicultural Support Teams to write a composite poem that captures each of their personal definitions of success.

   Each student says what success means to him or her, and then the teams weaves these thoughts together into a poem.

   Although they could write their poem in free verse, it might be more fun if they tried to make it rhyme.

4. When the teams are finished, have them read their poems to the rest of the class. You may want to have the poems printed on large paper to post in the classroom. The students could also draw on their posters to illustrate their poems of success.

Variation

Depending on how extensive a list of definitions of success were identified, you may want to extend this activity over a period of a few days. Before doing procedures 3 and 4, invite students to continue to explore what success means by paying attention to TV, interviewing family and friends, and so forth.

47 Success Collage

To follow, without halt, one aim: there's the secret of success.

—Anna Pavlova

Purpose

When you dream of success, what do you see? Do you imagine yourself winning the lottery? Do you see yourself in a position of power and influence? Do you have a picture of your ideal home and family? Or do you dream of making an enduring mark in the world or of being remembered for your contribution to humanity?

One secret to being successful is to have a clear picture of what success looks like for you. In the next two activities, your students will develop detailed pictures of what they want in the way of success and happiness.

Materials

heavy drawing paper (12″ × 18″)
magazines (including foreign language if possible)
scissors
glue or paste

Procedure

1. Distribute to students the drawing paper, magazines, scissors, and glue. They may work in Support Teams to share some of the materials.

2. Tell students to look through the magazines and find pictures of things that suggest what they personally think of as success and happiness.

3. Have students cut out pictures and glue them on the paper in designs that represent their personal views of success and happiness.

4. Suggest that they include words or phrases that fit into their designs. If there are other images they want to include that they can't find in magazines, they are free to draw these images.

5. When the students have completed their collages, have them take turns showing the others their collages and explaining how the designs illustrate their ideas of happiness and success. The other team members may ask questions if anything on a design seems unclear.

6. You may want to close the activity with a full-class discussion along the following lines: "Look again at the collage you created. Of all the images you used in the design, which is most important to you?"

7. You may want to invite your students to take their collages home and find time to discuss them with their parents. The collage can be used as a starting point for them to let their parents know what their current life goals are.

    You may also want to make the following suggestions: "Ask your parents to tell you what their goals were when they were your age. Then find out what they would like to see for your future. See if your goals and your parents' goals for you match."

8. Ask your students to bring the collages back to class so that they can be displayed on the bulletin board.

48 Success Visualization

*V*ictory won't come to me unless I go to it.
—Marianne Moore

Purpose

This activity supports students' success by having them imagine achieving their goals.

Procedure

1. Introduce the activity by saying:

   Today, you'll add some more detail to your picture of happiness and success. The collage you made during the previous activity included some of the symbols you identify with success and happiness. Today's imagination process lets you "put yourself in the picture" and feel what it's like to make your dreams come true.

2. Now read the following instructions for the eyes-closed imagination process:

   Please close your eyes, relax, and take a few deep breaths.

   Imagine walking down the hall to your favorite room, a room with all your favorite things in it . . .

   Imagine a place where you can sit comfortably to watch TV . . . a chair, sofa, bed, or pillows where you can fully relax and just watch your television. . . .

   You'll be spending a few minutes watching some pictures on the TV screen, so make sure that you have a good view. . . .

   With your remote control device, go ahead and turn on the TV and the VCR.

   Today you are going to watch a video entitled "Lifestyles of the Successful and Happy."

   As the video begins, you first see the pictures that you cut out of the magazine when you did your success and happiness collage.

   As you remember the images you found that represented being happy and successful, you now see these same images on the TV screen.

   Now you begin to see yourself on the TV amid these images of happiness and success.

If your pictures were of objects, you see yourself holding the objects.

If your pictures were of places, you see yourself in these places.

And if your pictures were of people, you see yourself with these people. (Pause.)

Now, you notice that the remote control of the VCR has a special button (very advanced technology): a 3-D button that will change the picture from being two-dimensional to being three-dimensional, so that you can actually walk around the objects . . . and see them from all sides...and touch them . . .

As you push the 3-D button, you experience yourself actually surrounded by your images of happiness and success.

As you interact with each of these things and people, you experience the happiness that you have interacting with other people . . . with your friends . . . and with your family.

The longer you do this, the more alive and real these pictures become for you.

Notice how you can easily project those feelings of happiness and success now . . .

Very good. Now bring into your experience the thoughts, emotions, and physical sensations that go along with being happy and successful, having achieved all your goals.

O.K., you'll have another minute now to just enjoy this experience before returning back here. (Wait one minute.)

As you realize that this experience of happiness and success is available to you at any time simply by coming to your special room and watching this special 3-D video, you also realize that it is time to leave now. Press the 3-D button on the remote control and switch back to sitting in the chair with the pictures on the TV. . . . Very good.

As you turn off the VCR and TV, you stand up and get ready to leave your favorite room for now. Remember, you can always return to this favorite room simply by closing your eyes. . . . But for now, imagine coming back into the hallway, walking back into this room. Recall what this room looks like, where you are, who else is here. Bring yourself into this room totally. Let yourself feel good about being here. When you know you are back in this room totally and feel good about being here, please open your eyes.

3. After the process, have your students join their Support Teams to share their experience. Suggest that they describe what they pictured about success and happiness during the eyes-closed process. Were there any surprises? What did it feel like to be that happy and successful?

49   Highlights of My Life—II

*Y*ou must do the thing you think you cannot do.
—Eleanor Roosevelt

Purpose

The purpose of this activity is for students to create a vision of what they would like to accomplish in the future.

Procedure

1. You could do this activity solely as a worksheet exercise, using the same process as Activity 15, only this time asking the students to project fifteen years into the future.

2. It could be done first as a guided imagination exercise.

3. Introduce the activity by explaining what students will be doing:

   This activity is an eyes-closed imagination process. You will be in your favorite room watching a video of your life as it might be in the future. It is an opportunity for you to begin creating a successful future for yourself.

4. Ask students to close their eyes, relax, and take a few deep breaths.

5. Continue with the following instructions:

   You find yourself walking down a hallway that feels like home.

   At the end of the hallway, you discover a room just like the one you've always wanted.

   As you enter the room, you notice the colors in the room—the walls, the floor, the furniture. You also notice that all your favorite things are in this room, and you realize this is really a perfect place to be.

   And now you decide to find a place where you can relax for a few minutes—maybe a comfortable chair or sofa, or perhaps a bed or a stack of pillows on the floor.

   As you get really comfortable, you decide to watch TV for awhile, and as you do, you notice a television set and you see that you have a good view of it from where you are sitting. . . . Very good!

   As the television comes on, you see the title of a movie, "Coming Attractions."

Your future is divided into three parts:

- *The next five years*
- *The five years after that*
- *The five years after that*

So you are reviewing the next fifteen years of your life. You'll be seeing the highlights of your life—the major events or accomplishments that will occur during this time. Some of the events you may experience are:

- *Completing elementary school and high school*
- *Getting your driver's license and being able to drive a car.*

And now, as you continue to look and listen, notice what events unfold in your life.

If the screen goes blank or isn't clear, that's O.K. Just ask yourself, "What will I accomplish in my life during the next five years?" and listen to the answers. Let it flow easily. As you do, you notice that you can see and hear many events you would like to have occur in the next five years. (Pause for two to four minutes.)

And now you find yourself drifting even further into the future. You are beginning to move on to the next five years—six to ten years from now. Excellent! Very good!

By now you have probably been in high school or have graduated from high school and have gone on to college or a full-time job. (Use age-appropriate information here.)

And, as you take your next breath, you begin to notice what high points might occur during this period of your life.

And, as I stop talking, you begin to see and hear what shows up on your screen. (Pause for two to four minutes.)

Very good. . . . As you let go of these images, you begin to find yourself moving on to the ten- to fifteen-year range, so you might notice in the mirror how you've gotten a little older. You may be surprised at how much older and more mature you look!

During this time frame, you will be approaching and maybe passing twenty years of age. What will you have accomplished by now?

- *Enjoying a significant relationship*
- *Living on your own*
- *Working at a new, more challenging job*
- *Maybe becoming famous for something*

Just let yourself continue to watch the screen and notice what you see ahead. (Pause for two to four minutes.)

Very good. Now, as you begin to let go of these sounds and images, you find your awareness leaving the television set and coming back to the room. You realize that for now the movie is over. There will be more to see later in the future, but it is time to leave now. So you get up and turn off the TV.

As you get ready to leave the room, you realize that you can always return here to go back to your future any time you want, simply by closing your eyes and walking down the hall, but for now it is time to leave.

As you leave and walk back down the hall, you realize what a gift it is to be clear about some of your visions for the future.

After awhile, you find yourself walking down the hallway to this classroom. As you enter the room, you take your seat and begin to notice how it feels to sit in your chair. You can feel your back against the back of the chair and your feet on the floor. As you notice the rising and falling of your chest and stomach as you breathe in and out, you become aware of the sounds around you in the room. You start to think about what this room looks like. When you have a clear sense of it, you slowly open your eyes and return your attention to the room.

6. Hand out copies of the Highlights of My Life—II Worksheet and have the students write or draw in the filmstrip frames images of their future success that they experienced during the fantasy.

7. Have the students share with partners or in their support groups.

8. Bring the entire class together for final comments.

Highlights of My Life—II Worksheet

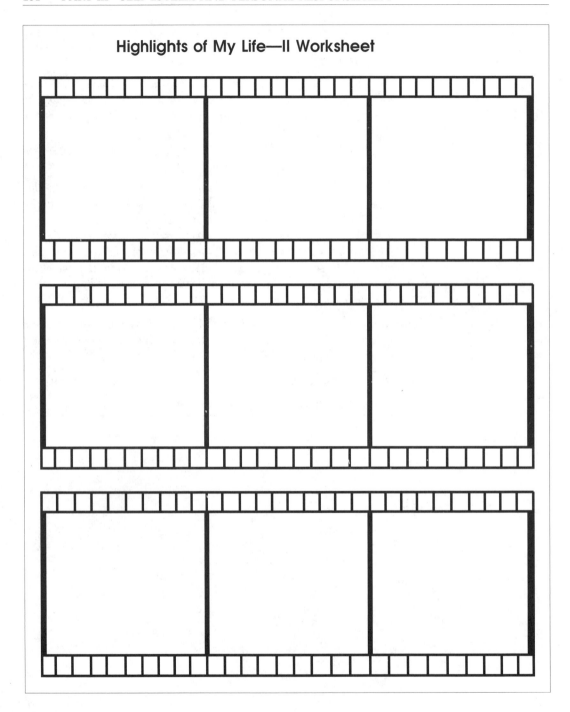

50   Give It Your Best Shot

*When we do the best that we can,
we never know what miracle is wrought in our life,
or in the life of another.*

—Helen Keller

Purpose

This activity gives students practice in setting goals and reaching them. The object of this game, unlike that of most games, is not necessarily to score the most points but to set realistic goals and achieve them. Athletic talent is not as important here as a good knowledge of one's abilities and a willingness to take a moderate risk. In other words, know what's possible, dream a little, and then go for it.

Materials

4 waste baskets

4 to 12 tennis balls (used tennis balls can usually be obtained free from a country club or tennis club)

masking tape

measuring tape or ruler

Procedure

1. In preparation for the activity, have the students place one waste basket in each corner of the room and measure 3 feet, 5 feet, and 10 feet away from the basket, using masking tape to mark these throw lines. Adjust the spacing depending on the age of the students.

2. Form four teams of equal size within the class, or use the Student Support Teams.

3. Supply each team with three tennis balls. The object of the game is to score the most points by getting the ball in the basket from the greatest distance possible, with as much accuracy as possible.

   If a student makes a basket from the first marker (a piece of masking tape 3 feet from the basket), he or she scores 5 points; from the second marker (5 feet from the basket), 10 points; and from the third marker (10 feet from the basket), 15 points. Before shooting, each student is to set a goal for how many points he or she intends to score.

4. On the first round, students will be practicing to see how skillful they are. They may take three shots from any distance. Using the results of this first round, they are to set a goal for the second round.

5. Before they start the second round, they are to state their goals—how many points they intend to score—using the Best Shot Worksheet.

6. After everyone has had a turn, have them pull their chairs together into a group and discuss what they learned about goal setting. Ask them to consider:

> "How well did you do in achieving your goal?"
>
> "If you made your goal, congratulate yourself."
>
> "Do you think you could have scored even more points if you had taken a little more risk?"
>
> "If you did not make your goal, what happened? Did you set your goal too high?"
>
> "What advice would you give to other players about how to score the maximum number of points?"

7. Give the students a few more rounds so that they can improve their ability to set realistic goals.

Best Shot Worksheet

	Round 1 (Practice)	Goal	Round 2 (Actual)
Ball 1	_____ Number of Points	_____	_____
Ball 2	_____	_____	_____
Ball 3	_____	_____	_____
Total	_____ Number of Points	_____	_____

51 Crossing the Goal Line

It is not enough to aim, you must hit.

—Italian Proverb

Purpose

This activity will encourage your students to take action on their goals and to keep track of their accomplishments.

Materials

For this activity, you will need to make a large bulletin board on which to display the students' goal markers. Make the bulletin board look like a football or soccer field with a line at the left for the starting line and another at the right for the goal line. Divide the field into 10-yard marks to make 100 yards.

Have students make their goal markers and pin them at the starting line. Each day that students meet their goals, the markers are advanced 20 yards toward the goal line. Their goal markers may be index cards with the names and/or photographs of the students on them, or they may be cut in the shape of footballs or shapes unique and special to each student.

Procedure

1. Introduce the activity to your class as follows:

   Did you ever wonder why they call it the goal line? It's because the goal line is where you score points. If you want to score points in achieving your goals, you have to keep track of what your goals are.

2a. One way to set up this activity is as a weekly check-in, following up on "Report Card Affirmation" (Activity 54). Have students pick one of the subject areas that they are looking to achieve a certain grade. The desired final grade is posted at the goal line and weekly grades for assignments, quizzes, tests, and so forth get posted so that students know from week to week how well they are progressing toward their goal. Many schools are moving away from letter grades to more authentic means of assessment such as portfolios. In this case, the goal could be the actual product rather than the grade.

2b. The activity could also be a daily check toward a one-week goal. To do this, select an area of study such as spelling or vocabulary words, multiplication tables or fractions, or any project where progress can be measured—number of pages read, number of problems completed, sections of the report finished, and so forth.

3. Prepare goal markers indicating where students will be at the end of the week or the end of the grading period. The weekly goals may be individualized on the basis of each student's current level of success in this area, or the goal could be uniform for the entire class.

   Place these markers on the right side of the bulletin board on the goal line.

4. Hand out a blank goal marker to the students and ask them to think about what they could accomplish today that would move them closer to the Goal Line, or what grade they intend to get this week that would get them to their desired final goals. Have them write this short-term goal on their card. For example, if the week's goal is to read 25 pages in a particular book, then the goal for today could be finishing the next 5 pages. If the semester goal is to get a B in math, then the goal for this week is to get at least a B on the quiz.

   Also, have the students state what strategies or actions they will take to achieve their short-term goal—for example, study 30 minutes each day, come in before class for extra help, and so forth.

5. Have each student read his or her goal for today or for the week as well as the action steps, go to the bulletin board, and post the card at the starting line.

6. Each day for a week or each week for the grading period, have the students report on their success with short-term goals. They are to move their markers 20 yards for each time they are successful.

7. If certain students are not succeeding, you may want to provide them with support in identifying what is happening. Do this in a nonjudgmental manner, looking to discover the facts of the situation.

   Perhaps the goal was unrealistic and needs to be modified, or maybe aspects of it are beyond the student's control. Maybe they didn't follow through on the action steps. You may use the Coaching Questions for Achieving Goals and Coaching Questions for Completing Assignments on the following pages as ways of structuring your interactions with students.

8. If some students are coming in with excuses for not completing their goals, the next activity will help you address these.

9. When a student gets to the goal line, plan some sort of acknowledgment or celebration, such as a standing ovation from the class, a small prize, a note home, or whatever you and your students decide.

Coaching Questions for Achieving Goals

1. What was the goal you set for yourself?

2. Did you achieve it?

3. *If yes:* congratulations!
   - What specifically did you do?
   - To what do you owe your success?
   - How do you feel about your accomplishment?
   - What worked for you in support of your success?
   - What did you learn from this?
   - Were there any points along the way that were difficult and/or where things didn't work?
   - What did you learn from this?
   - Would you say this goal was too easy, too difficult, challenging yet realistic, or enough of a stretch to be a real accomplishment?
   - Given your experience, what is your goal for the next period of time?

   If no:
   - What happened?
   - How do you feel about what happened?
   - In what way was this what you expected?
   - What happened that was unexpected?
   - What didn't work?
   - What did you learn from this?
   - Were there points along the way when you were successful?
   - What worked?
   - What did you learn from this?
   - What are the consequences of your not having achieved your goal?
   - Commitment check—On a scale of 1 to 10, how committed would you say you were?
   - Is this goal still important to you?
   - What is your purpose in accomplishing this?
   - Given your experience this time, how will you modify your goal?
   - What will you do differently in achieving the goal?
   - What other resources or support do you feel you need?
   - Commitment check—On a scale of 1 to 10, how committed would you say you are now to accomplishing this goal?

Coaching Questions for Completing Assignments

1. What were your assignments?

2. Did you complete them all?

3. *If yes:*

   - How did you feel about it?
   - What supported you in keeping your commitment?
   - What did you learn about yourself?

   If no:

   - Did you make a commitment to do your assignments?
   - What happened that you didn't do them?
   - What was more important to you than keeping your word?
   - How do you feel about that?
   - What did you learn about yourself in the process?
   - What will you do differently in the future?

52 Favorite Excuses

We are all manufacturers—making good, making trouble or making excuses.

—H. V. Adolt

Purpose

This activity helps students to realize that they can either have what they want in life (their goals), or have the excuses for why they don't have what they want.

"The dog ate my homework."
"The car broke down."
"My mother didn't wake me up in time."
"Somebody stole my pencil."
"Nobody told me!"

Do you recognize these? They are famous favorite excuses that every kid learns along with the ABCs. Everybody has a sackful of excuses, good for any occasion. What's your excuse? (And don't try to use the excuse that you couldn't think of an excuse!)

Materials

Post-it® pads

Procedure

1. Have the students bring their chairs into a class circle.

2. Give them each a stack of Post-it® notes.

3. Tell them that they are going to be writing excuses on the Post-it® notes, one excuse per note.

4. Instruct them as follows:

> "First write all the excuses you can think of for not getting your homework done. Remember, one excuse per note."
>
> "Next, write all the excuses you know for not getting to school on time."
>
> "Now all the excuses for not taking out the garbage."
>
> "Now all the ones for not cleaning your room."
>
> "All the excuses you have for not liking yourself."
>
> "All the excuses you have for others not liking you."
>
> "All the excuses for not doing well in school."
>
> "All the excuses for not finishing your twenty-four-hour goal."

5. Go around the circle and have students read off their favorite excuses. Post them on a "Favorite Excuses" bulletin board.

6. You may want to explore with your students what motivates people to settle for the excuse rather than succeed at a goal. What purpose does excuse-making serve?

    Sometimes excuses are ways we have of protecting ourselves. We protect ourselves from the discomfort of feeling like a failure if we have a good excuse for not having met our goal. We can avoid the fear of punishment if we can convince our parents that we had a good enough reason for not doing what we were told. We can save face with our friends if we can blame our parents for not letting us stay out all night.

7. In the future, when a student gives an excuse for something, you can simply point to the "Favorite Excuses" bulletin board and suggest that

it is not necessary to make up a new one—that we already have plenty from which to pick. Remind them that *you can have what you want (your goal) or you can have the excuses for why you don't.*

Note: This activity often raises the question as to whether there are ever legitimate excuses. The term excuse *is being used here to describe those times when people settle for less than they are capable of achieving and point to something outside themselves as the reason why.*

The activity is meant to challenge that mind set in order to empower students by having them realize they need not be limited by circumstances. In this sense, it is related to Activity 44, "From Victim to Victor." The key is personal responsibility. Sometimes, I deliberately choose to do something other than what I said I would do. ("My grandmother came to visit, and I chose to spend time with her rather than do my homework. My relationships goal became more important than my achievement goal. I chose it. I am not making an excuse for myself. I am willing to accept the consequences of my actions.")

Other times, circumstances beyond my control prevent me from achieving what I set out to do. ("I agreed to meet you at 4:00 P.M. to play ball, and the bus was late. When I made the agreement, I didn't plan for such an eventuality. Knowing what I know about public transportation, I should have left earlier, arranged for other transportation, or told you 4:30 P.M. instead. I apologize for keeping you waiting. In the future, I'll plan better.") Again, responsibility leads to empowerment.

53   I Can't/I Haven't Yet

If you think you can, you can. And if you think you can't, you're right.

—Mary Kay Ash

Purpose

To support students in realizing how language affects their perception and how they can use responsible statements to empower themselves.

Procedure

1. Ask the students to find partners. Have them take turns saying sentences that feel true for them that start with the words "I can't . . ."—for example, "I can't learn to do math," "I can't remember my times tables," "I can't get to school on time," "I can't make any friends." Ask

them to consider their school life, their social life, their home life, and so on as possible areas from which to draw these statements.

2. After about two minutes, ask them to go back and repeat all the sentences they have just said with one change: replacing the word *can't* with the words *haven't yet*, as in "I haven't yet learned how to do math," "I haven't yet remembered my times tables," and so forth.

    Ask them to repeat exactly what they said before, except for the substitution of *haven't yet* for *can't*, and to take the time to be aware of how they experience saying each sentence. Ask them to notice if it feels any different and, if it does, to remember *how* it feels different. Again, give them about two minutes to do this.

3. Bring the class back together and ask them what they experienced as they did the exercise. Did they experience any difference between saying "I can't" and saying "I haven't yet"?

4. Ask them to consider whether their "I can't" statements are really statements of something that is impossible, or whether it is something possible that they simply have not yet done. "I can't" implies being unable, limited, and controlled from the outside. "I haven't yet" creates the possibility that it can happen now or sometime in the future.

5. After you have used this exercise with your class, make a habit of correcting people in class who say, "I can't." Ask them to repeat whatever they have said with the words "I haven't yet."

54 Report Card Affirmation

Background

Affirmations are positive statements that affirm or declare a desired objective as if it were already achieved. The purpose of an affirmation is to build "structural tension" or "cognitive dissonance" in the brain, which thereby creates the internal motivation to take the actions necessary to achieve a goal. This structural tension can be further increased by using the affirmation in conjunction with a clear visual image of the desired outcome.

Whenever the mind simultaneously holds two realities that do not match, cognitive dissonance occurs. If your current reality is that you are a poor student and you affirm and visualize being an excellent student, then you will experience structural tension. If you deliberately create and hold this structural tension in your mind on a daily basis, it will intensify and create the following mental changes:

- You will begin to experience creative ideas that will help you achieve your goal.

- You will start to perceive all kinds of internal and external resources to help you achieve your goal that you were never aware of before now. Your awareness will expand to take in new data to help you.

- You will experience increased motivation to take action.

All motivation comes from having a picture of something you want that does not match the picture of what you have. The more you can increase the interplay between those two images, the more you will increase your motivation. Affirmations, which are word pictures describing the completed goal, help elicit visual pictures, thereby increasing the structural tension and motivation.

The beliefs, expectations, and thought patterns that your students currently hold also determine their self-esteem, and how willing they are to participate in school and in life. If students believe that they are slow learners, poor students, not mathematically inclined, physically awkward, or stupid, then that is what they will create. The belief and the picture will create the future and will control their actions.

Students can learn to use affirmations to override their self-defeating beliefs. They can transform their internal experience of themselves, and then gradually modify their daily behavior to match their new beliefs.

Purpose

This exercise works on the principle of cognitive dissonance applied to students' academic achievement. The purpose is to motivate students to improve their performance, whether measured by grades or by some other means of assessment.

Materials

blank report card forms (14 per student)
an envelope for each student

Procedure

1. Give each student 14 blank report card forms.

2. Instruct each student to take one copy of the form and write down all the necessary information: his or her name, classes, teachers, and so on.

3. In cases where grades are used, have the students think about what grades they would like to see on their report cards. Make the point that the grades don't necessarily have to be straight A's. Tell your students to write in the grades they want to see on their report cards—"the grade you believe you actually are capable of earning at this point."

4. If the form of assessment is something other than grades and report cards, then discuss with your students how their performance will be measured, what skills they are expected to learn, what projects they will be expected to complete, and what products will be used to evaluate their progress. Supply students with copies of whatever assessment tool they will actually be receiving, and tell them to fill in the performance objectives they intend to accomplish.

5. Have them bring their completed report cards or assessment forms with them to share with the entire group.

6. After students have shown their report cards or assessment forms to the class, ask them to agree to repeat this activity—writing out forms with the grades or alternative measures of success they want to see on their next performance record—twice a day for the next five days.

7. Have the students put a copy of their completed form in an envelope and address it to themselves. Collect these envelopes for safekeeping. At the end of the reporting period, return the forms to the students and discuss the process.

> *Intelligence is characterized by a natural inability to understand.*
> —Henri Bergson

55 Using All My Smarts

> *Even the best needles are not sharp at both ends.*
> —Chinese proverb

Background

As public schools struggle to serve an increasingly diverse student population, a growing number of youngsters are identified as being "at risk." An alternative view is that it is the schools, not the students, that are "at risk"— at risk of failing to provide for the needs of their clients. Shifting the focus in this way challenges schools to find alternatives for serving all students, not just those who are able to adapt to the existing educational pedagogy and methodology.

For example, most schools favor a mode of instruction that is individualistic and highly competitive. European American males tend to have an advantage in this type of environment, whereas females and members of other cultural groups are more likely to succeed in a cooperative group setting.

Recognizing that students have different learning styles is a necessary first step in transforming "at risk" schools. Many different theories of learning styles exist and the exact way in which culture, ethnicity, social class, and child-rearing practices influence learning styles is not completely clear. However, using a range of different teaching styles in order to engage students in a manner that is likely to be compatible with their style of learning is an obvious approach that holds great promise.

Howard Gardner's work on multiple intelligences, though not specifically related to cultural differences, is one theory that has important implications because it goes beyond the limited definition of intelligence valued in most schools.

According to Gardner, people are capable of processing information, solving problems, and developing products in several different ways—each of which could be said to be a specific "intelligence." These include:

- **Verbal/Linguistic:** Referring to the use of words and language, both written and spoken, this intelligence is the basis for reading, writing, abstract reasoning, symbolic thinking, and so forth. The curricula of most Western educational systems are dominated by this way of knowing.

- **Logical/Mathematical:** This is the other predominant intelligence emphasized in most schools. The number skills of the mathematician and the reasoning skills of the scientist are included in this domain.

- **Visual/Spatial:** The sense of sight is key to this intelligence. The ability to visualize objects from different perspectives and create mental pictures is among the skills that are important to artists, designers, architects, and others who have strengths in this type of intelligence.

- **Body/Kinesthetic:** Athletes and dancers are examples of people who are skilled in this area. "Learning by doing" is the best way to teach the kinesthetic learner.

- **Musical/Rhythmic:** Music and rhythm are sometimes used to teach younger children, as with the ABCs jingle. According to advocates of "Super Learning," a particular type of background music enhances student ability to learn foreign languages or retain factual information. Composers and musicians exemplify people with skills in this area.

- **Interpersonal:** This intelligence supports the ability to be effective in dealing with other people. Communication, cooperation, and compassion are among the skills of people such as teachers, counselors, and therapists, who have strengths in this area.

- **Intrapersonal:** Philosophers perhaps best reflect this intelligence, which involves knowledge of the internal aspects of oneself, such as observing emotional states and thinking processes, as well as an awareness of spiritual realities.

Purpose

The aim of this activity is to have students become aware of the different ways of knowing. Students who are adept at intelligences that are typically undervalued in schools will feel validated.

In addition, you may feel excited about the challenge of planning your lessons with the seven intelligences* in mind so that all students have an opportunity to build on their strengths.

Procedure

1. Have students get into their Support Teams and give them copies of the All My Smarts Worksheet I.

2. Ask them to identify students within their team who are good at the skills that are listed on the worksheet. Students may mention their own names as well as those of their teammates.

3. Bring the class together. Review each cluster of strengths and have each team mention students in their group who have these skills.

    Write each skill on the board and put in the names or initials of students who are strong in these areas.

    After each cluster of skills, identify the area of intelligence to which these belong by writing the heading on the board.

4. Next, give each student a copy of All My Smarts Worksheet II and ask them to color in the parts that show their strengths—estimating how fully developed each skill is. Starting at the center of the circle, have them fill in as much of each section as they feel they have this particular set of skills. Some of the students, for example, may fill in almost all

---

*For further discussion of multiple intelligences as the concept relates to educational practices, read *Seven Ways of Teaching* and *Seven Ways of Knowing*, both by David Lazear (Palatine, IL: Skylight Publishing, 1991).

of the athlete wedge, half of the musician wedge, and 10 percent of the scientist wedge.

5. Now have the students pick one of the type of intelligences that is less developed and make a goal to increase their skill in this area. Discuss with your students what they have already learned from previous activities about achieving goals that they can apply to this area. (See Activities 47–52.)

6. Make the point that each student has a different set of strengths and that we can learn from each other. Invite the students to mill around the classroom talking to their classmates, comparing their All My Smarts Worksheet II charts. Have each student find a "mentor"—someone who is strong in the area in which they are weak (targeted as a goal to be developed).

7. Give them time to meet with their mentor to discuss ways in which to improve in this area.

8. Reinforce the relationship by providing time over the next few days and weeks for students to meet with their mentors.

9. In about two weeks, have the mentors present their protégés and share with the rest of the class what progress the student has made.

10. Have the students update their charts on the All My Smarts Worksheet II.

All My Smarts Worksheet I

Author   *Skill Set 1* _____   *Student's Name*

- reading/vocabulary   _____
- creative writing/poetry   _____
- speaking/humor   _____

Scientist   *Skill Set 2* _____   *Student's Name*

- math   _____
- outlining   _____
- figuring out codes and puzzles   _____

Artist   *Skill Set 3* _____   *Student's Name*

- art   _____
- color/design   _____
- vivid imagination   _____

Athlete   *Skill Set 4* _____   *Student's Name*

- sports/martial arts   _____
- dance/mime   _____
- inventing   _____

Musician   *Skill Set 5* _____   *Student's Name*

- singing   _____
- music   _____
- vocal sounds   _____

Counselor   *Skill Set 6* _____   *Student's Name*

- communication   _____
- cooperative learning   _____
- caring about others   _____

Philosopher   *Skill Set 7* _____   *Student's Name*

- self-reflection   _____
- focus/concentration   _____
- spirituality   _____

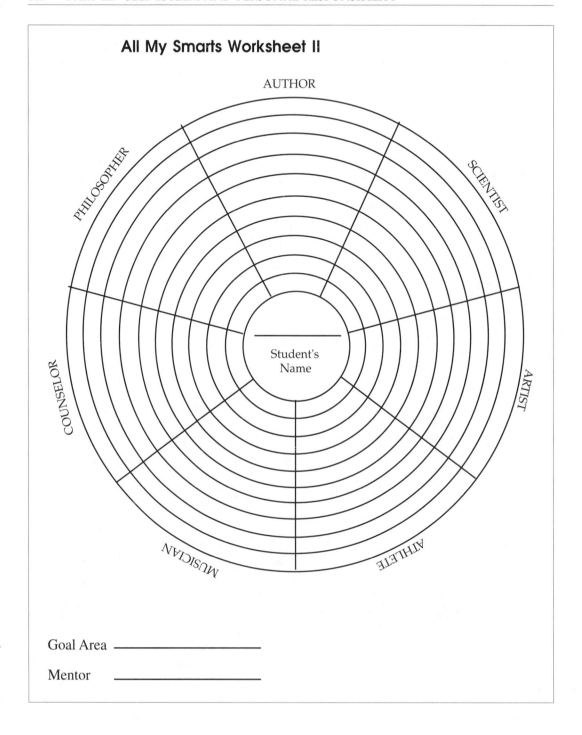

All My Smarts Worksheet II

AUTHOR

PHILOSOPHER

SCIENTIST

COUNSELOR

ARTIST

MUSICIAN

ATHLETE

Student's Name

Goal Area _____

Mentor _____

56   Captain Self-Esteem

*Y*ou ask me why I do not write something . . . I think
one's feelings waste themselves in words, they ought all
to be distilled into actions and into actions which bring
results.

—Florence Nightingale

Anecdotal Material

Like Parts I and II, this section, which has focused on empowerment and achievement, ends with a video-recording activity.

This activity was done with a group of high school students. They were told that other teachers in the school were curious about what these students were learning in the self-esteem program, and so they decided to produce a video that could be used to communicate what we had been doing. They were given thirty minutes to prepare.

When the students returned—lights, camera, action!

The students role-played being at a party. Each of them had a sign indicating how he or she was feeling—bored, lonely, sad, upset, and so forth—as they acted out these feelings.

After much complaining and negative commentary, someone finally said, "This looks like a job for Captain Self-Esteem." In came a hefty young man with a big "S" on his shirt to save the day.

As Captain Self-Esteem touched each of the students, they turned their signs around—bored changed to having fun, lonely became friendly, sad turned to happy, and so forth—and proceeded to act consistent with these positive feelings.

The selection of this particular student as Captain Self-Esteem—however the students decided on it—was brilliant because he was the member of the group most in need of learning to value himself and experience the acceptance of others.

Purpose

To support students in integrating the key learnings of this section by asking them to apply their knowledge in some type of presentation.

Materials

video recorder and playback equipment
blank video tape

Procedure

1. Let students know that we have come to the end of another section of the program, and that it is time for the next episode in their TV series.

Creative Approach

2. Hand out the Part III—Key Learnings and discuss the points that were covered in these two chapters. Have the students vote on the one or more ideas they would like to use in this activity.

3. Review the list of types of television programs from Activity 17 and, with your students, decide what form to use in relation to the topics selected.

4. Give them time to work on the concept, write the script, make props, rehearse, and so forth.

5. Proceed to step 10.

Structured Approach

2. Borrowing the idea from the students mentioned in the Anecdotal Material, tell your students that the title of the TV episode is "Captain Self-Esteem."

3. Brainstorm with your students a list of words describing how people feel when they don't have any self-esteem, don't feel empowered, or don't feel successful.

4. Next, have students identify words that describe how people feel when they do have self-esteem. A good way of doing this would be to have the negative feeling in one column and the opposite, positive feeling in a column next to it.

5. Have each student select one of the pairs of words (*sad/happy, upset/calm,* and so forth) that they would be willing to act out. Have them make signs with the negative word on one side and the positive word on the other. The signs should be large enough to be read by the camera.

6. Describe the setup: students in a group acting out low self-esteem behaviors; "Captain Self-Esteem" arrives and zaps them with power and confidence; group changes to high self-esteem behaviors.

7. Ask students for suggestions as to how to pick who will play "Captain Self-Esteem." Possible ways of choosing might include:

   • One student volunteers and no one else wants to do it, and everyone is comfortable with his or her having this role.

- If there is more than one volunteer, then they could audition for the part and students could vote on who did the best job.
- You could use random selection.

8. Have the group decide on what type of a setting they want to create for the scene—at a party, in a classroom, at a ball game, outside on the playground, and so forth.

9. Give students some time to work together in small groups discussing what kinds of behaviors are appropriate for the ''before'' and ''after'' scenes. You are likely to have more students than pairs of words, so more than one student can act out *sad/happy*, for example. You could have students with the same pair of words get together to plan different ways of acting out the part.

10. Do a dress rehearsal and have students offer constructive feedback for how to make it even better.

11. Video tape it and play it back.

12. Discuss with the students whether or not they would like to show the video to anyone else.

13. Complete the activity with a discussion on what the students have learned so far in the program.

Low Self-Esteem Feelings and Actions	*High Self-Esteem Feelings and Actions*
mad	glad
sad	happy
upset	calm
lonely	friendly
bored	excited, having fun
victim	victor
complaining	complementing
withdrawing	participating
arguing	communicating
failing	succeeding
making excuses	excelling

Part III—Key Learnings

I am capable of being
anything
I want to be.

I am getting
what I want rather
than settling for excuses.

I am able to move from
victim to victor

It is not that I can't,
I just haven't yet.

I am powerful.

I am smart.

I have the power
to succeed.

I am achieving
my goals.

Part III—Teacher Checklist:
Creating a Multicultural Environment That Builds the Self-Esteem of Students

❏   Am I tailoring my curriculum so that it is relevant to my students—their interests and ambitions as well as their cultural identity?

❏   Am I aware of my students' various learning styles, and do my teaching strategies reflect this awareness?

❏   Are the books and other materials I use reflective of diversity—ethnicity, culture, race, class, gender, age, handicapping conditions, and so forth?

❏   Are the images on the walls, bulletin boards, and so forth also reflective of diversity?

❏   Are a variety of family groupings, life-styles, and types of homes represented in my classroom materials?

❏   Are the materials in my classroom nonsexist—showing both males and females in nurturing roles and depicting a variety of occupational roles and interest areas as being equally appropriate for girls and boys?

❏   How is the seating arrangement consistent with my educational objectives, and how does it support all students in learning most effectively?

❏   Have I provided opportunities for my students to help maintain the classroom environment so as to encourage their sense of responsibility?

❏   Were the students involved in developing class rules (operating instructions, protocol, or agreements) so that they feel ownership for them?

❏   Do I give my students opportunities to make choices in appropriate areas as a way of letting them exercise responsibility?

❏   Have all my students set goals for themselves, and am I providing effective coaching that may be different for each child but equally empowering for all of them?

❏   Have I embraced the idea of multicultural education to the point that it has become part of the very fabric of our classroom culture?

Chapter 6—Suggested Student Readings

Cummings, Pat. *Jimmy Lee Did It.* New York: Lothrop, 1985.

Dobrin, Arnold. *Josephine's Magination.* New York: Scholastic, 1975.

Dr. Seuss. *Horton Hatches the Egg.* New York: Random House, 1940.

Felt, Susan. *Rosa Too Little.* New York: Doubleday, 1950.

Little, Lessie, & Eloise Greenfield. *I Can Do It Myself.* New York: Crowell, 1978.

Martin, Bill, Jr., & John Archambault. *Knots on a Counting Rope.* Allen, TX: DCM, 1989.

Shah, Idries. *World Tales.* New York: Harcourt Brace Jovanovich, 1979.

Uchida, Yoshiko. *Sumi's Prize.* New York: Scribner's, 1964.

Wisniewski, David. *Rain Player.* New York: Clarion Books, 1991.

Part IV

Self-Esteem and Social Responsibility

Making the World Work

How wonderful it is that nobody need wait a single moment before starting to improve the world.
—Anne Frank

	Experience (Internal)	Express (External)
Others	Interdependence	Social Responsibility
Self	Independence	Personal Responsibility

Chapter 7

Collaboration

Can't We All Get Along?

A generous heart feels others' ills
as if it were responsible for them.
—Vauvenargues

Introduction

*W*e didn't all come over on the same ship
but we're all in the same boat.
—Bernard M. Baruch

"Chrissy's House. Keep Out!" the sign said.

It was a terrific tree house, too. Painted bright blue with red shutters it even had a porch where you could sit. Inside were a table and chair and a rug with a couple of fat pillows.

When Leah, the girl who lived next door, asked if she could come up and see the tree house, Chrissy said, "No. It's just for me."

"Leah's House. Keep Out."

Leah's tree house was built in a day. Made from old wood, it was crooked and had holes in it. It was not painted and didn't have shutters. Chrissy knew hers was better.

Maybe on the outside, agreed Leah, but not in the inside.

For several days the two girls sat alone in their tree houses not speaking to each other. When Chrissy had finished reading all her books—some more than once—she asked Leah if she could borrow some. Upon learning that Leah didn't have any books at all to read, Chrissy offered to let her read hers.

"I could come visit you . . . or you could come visit me."
They found a wide board that could connect the two porches and Chrissy thought that the best part of their tree houses was not the shutters or the pillows but the bridge.
"WELCOME" was what both their signs said now.*

Stereotypes, prejudices, and discrimination are ways in which people from one group keep themselves separate from and better than another group. Such attitudes and behaviors are based on ignorance, insecurity, and fear. Being on the receiving end of prejudice diminishes one's sense of self-worth, especially if it plays into the recipient's fears and insecurities.

This chapter emphasizes the importance of all us working together. We must all learn to cooperate rather than compete and to move beyond conflict to collaboration.

Students will learn to communicate better—especially to listen to others' viewpoints. They will learn to trust each other and to solve problems together. In this way we can replace ignorance with knowledge, insecurity with confidence, and fear with love.

It is incumbent upon us as educators to model effective communication and listening skills. As the saying goes, "Students don't care how much we know until they know how much we care." One of the best ways to show we care is to really listen so that students feel heard.

Communication styles vary among cultural groups, and it is important to be sensitive to these differences. I once observed an interaction between an urban elementary school principal who was admonishing a young African-American child. The boy had his eyes cast downward as he listened to the principal's harsh words.

Misunderstanding the child's stance, the principal, a Caucasian of Greek descent, grabbed the boy's chin and demanded that he look at him while he was speaking. The two different cultures had opposite ways of showing respect.

Cultural rules related to communication, such as those listed here, are offered as general guidelines and are not meant to stereotype any particular group. Treating each person as an individual is always the best approach. You may want to discuss these guidelines with your students to see if they are consistent with their own experiences and to explore with them other behaviors that are appropriate in cross-cultural interactions.

- *Eye contact:* Direct eye contact is not consistent with cultural norms for many African Americans and Hispanics.

---

*"The Tree House" by Lois Lowry in *The Big Book of Peace*, ed. Ann Durrell and Marilyn Sachs (New York: Dutton, 1990).

- *Proximity:* How close people stand when talking to each other varies from culture to culture.

- *Taking turns:* Italian households often find family members talking at the same time, and many African Americans show they are listening by jumping in to agree or disagree as others are speaking.

- *Touching:* Some cultures are comfortable with physical contact as part of their communication style. Others, such as persons from the Middle East, for example, might not consider touching appropriate.

- *Loudness and tempo:* Speed of delivery, volume, and degree of emotionality vary among cultures. Many people, including some Native American societies, value silence and contemplation and do not feel compelled to respond to every statement made during a conversation.

57   SHARE to Show You Care

Caring is everything; nothing matters but caring.
—The last words of Baron Friedrich Von Hugel

Purpose

The need for attention is often pointed to as the source of many childhood behaviors—especially inappropriate ones. So to give students an opportunity to receive attention, to be really listened to, contributes greatly to their sense of belonging.

The purpose of this activity is for students to develop effective listening skills. These skills will be practiced over and over again in the activities that follow.

Procedure

1. Hand out the SHARE Worksheet and discuss these listening skills with your students. Ask students for examples and do some age-appropriate role plays to be sure that the guidelines are understood. For instance:

   - To demonstrate **S**: Be Still. Be Silent.
     Have a student come up to the front of the room and tell you about one of his or her favorite movies. While the student is talking, interupt with comments about your own favorite movie.

- To demonstrate **R**: Restate.
  This time have the student tell you about his or her favorite movie. At appropriate intervals, restate what the student has been saying to check for accuracy.

2. Hand out copies of the Share the Wealth Worksheet.

3. Describe the simulated situation to the students. The class has just received a donation of $100 from a wealthy member of the community. Their task is to decide how to spend the $100. The worksheet specifies the available options. Each team (Multicultural Support Team) has 20 minutes to reach a consensus on how to spend the money. If they are unable to decide within that time frame, the money will be given to another class instead.

4. The team agreement is that before any student can state his or her point of view, he or she must restate the point made by the person who spoke just before him or her. The students are to SHARE—to show they care—following the guidelines for effective listening.

5. Have each group select a moderator who will be in charge of making sure that everyone follows the agreements. This student will not otherwise get involved in the discussion.

6. Give a two-minute warning before the end of the time period, and then call time at the end of the 20 minutes.

7. Have someone from each team report on what option the group chose and the process used to arrive at it.

8. Engage the entire class in a discussion of effective listening skills and how they affect group process.

   - In what ways was it helpful?
   - Were there times when it got in the way?
   - How can these skills be applied in other areas of their lives?

From listening comes wisdom,
and from speaking repentance.

—Italian proverb

Share Worksheet: Effective Listening Skills

S

SHHHHHHHH!
BE **S**TILL. BE **S**ILENT.

H

HEAR WHAT THEY ARE SAYING.
HEAR WHAT THEY MEAN.

A

PAY **A**TTENTION. **A**LLOW THEM TO SPEAK.
ACCEPT WHAT THEY SAY AS TRUE FOR THEM.

R

RESTATE WHAT YOU HEARD THEM SAY TO BE
SURE YOU GOT THE MESSAGE.

E

ENCOURAGE THEM TO SPEAK.
MAKE IT **E**ASY FOR THEM TO SAY WHAT THEY
WANT.

*One of the best ways to persuade others
is with your ears—by listening to them.*

—Dean Rusk

58 Share the Wealth

Your class has received a $100 donation from a wealthy member of the community. As a group, you must decide on how to spend the money from among the options listed below.

You have 20 minutes to come to a decision; otherwise, the money will be given to another class. Your group must all agree on the choice.

Options:

1. Divide the money equally among all the class members.

2. Use the money to pay for a field trip related to a class project.

3. Give the money to the physical education department for more sports equipment.

4. Use the money to buy toys for a program like Toys for Tots for children less fortunate than yourselves.

5. Donate the money to an organization that provides meals for AIDS patients who are not well enough to care for themselves.

6. Use the money to buy blankets and distribute them to people who are homeless.

7. Use the money to set up a recycling program to help save the environment.

8. Spend the money on a fun party for your class.

59 Creating Our Own Culture: Name That Team

*C*ulture is both an intellectual phenomenon
and a moral one.

—Raisa M. Gorbachev

Purpose

This exercise is used to help students feel greater ownership for their team and a sense of identity with it.

Procedure

1. Remind students of what constitutes a culture (Activity 22) that it is a group's way of meeting their human needs by surviving in and adapting to their environment. Ask them to brainstorm with you the different aspects of a culture such as language, food, music, as well as values, beliefs, myths and so forth.

   Continue the discussion by explaining that businesses also use the term *culture* as in *corporate culture,* to define itself. Corporate culture refers to the company's name, image (refer to Activity 7, "Brand Names"), values, and ways of doing business.

   Next, refer to sports teams—both school and professional—that also try to create a culture with a name, an image or mascot, particular colors, and sometimes a song or cheer. This is designed to build loyalty among both players and fans.

   Ask students to identify their favorite teams and aspects of their culture—for example, Los Angeles Raiders (black and silver—pirate logo); New Orleans Saints (gold and black—fleur de lis logo); Boston Celtics (green and white—leprechaun logo).

   Let the students know that they are now going to create their own team culture.

2. Invite the students to move into their Multicultural Support Teams.

3. Tell them team members should agree on a name for their team. The name must be one that everyone on the team feels good about.

4. Remind them of their team agreements and ask them to use effective listening skills, SHARE, to be sure everyone is heard.

5. Suggest that they follow these steps:

   a. Discuss and agree on what positive characteristics of their team they want their name to convey. For example:

      "Bears" suggests strength
      "Cougars," speed
      "Giants," power

      One way to help students identify possible characteristics is to have them do "If You Were . . . ," Activity 10.

   b. Brainstorm all the possible names that could be used to communicate this quality. Consider names that take into account the multicultural makeup of the group.

   c. Discuss the advantages and disadvantages of each name and select the one that works best. Again, everyone on the team must accept the name that is chosen.

   d. Discuss how the "official" team name should look—printed or cursive, all caps or upper and lower case, and so forth—and where it can be used—book covers, T-shirts, next to students' names on class assignments, and so forth.

6. When the teams are finished, have each one make a presentation to the rest of the class describing their team name and how they came to choose it.

7. On subsequent days, use the same procedure to have Student Teams decide on:

   - Team colors
   - Team logo or mascot
   - Team handshake or greeting
   - Team song, anthem, cheer, or yell
   - Team motto

60 Team Trust Walk

*You may be deceived if you trust too much, but
you will live in torment unless you trust enough.*
—Dr. Frank Crane

Purpose

Trust is an essential quality for being in a relationship or part of a community. This exercise is designed to increase students' ability to trust and be trusted. By trusting others, we empower each other and allow ourselves to become even more worthy of trust.

Materials

This activity can be done by having students shut their eyes, or you can provide one blindfold (6" × 8" strip of cloth) for every student.

Procedure

1. For this activity you will need to find a suitable area of the school. You will need a space large enough for the class to move around freely in teams without running into each other or other students. You also need some privacy from outsiders who might disrupt the activity. The space should have some variation in terrain—some slopes or stairs, different surfaces to walk on, and so on. However, it should not have any dangerous areas where students could be injured. Ideally, the area would be open enough for you to observe the teams as they walk. If no one area is large enough, delegate students to be stationed in each area so that they can monitor the activity. Ideal places are the playground, a gymnasium, or a quiet wing of the school building.

2. Have the students get into their Support Teams. Let them know that they will be going on a "trust walk." Everyone on the team is blindfolded (or has his or her eyes closed) except the leader.

   Each student places his or her right hand on the right shoulder of the person in front. The student at the head of the line is the leader. He or she is not blindfolded and, without talking, leads the team on the walk. The leader seeks to make the walk fun and interesting, but not dangerous. The students lined up behind the leader get nonverbal cues from the movements of the person in front of them.

3. Before starting on the walk, discuss the risk factor and ask the students to communicate to their teammates any concerns they have.

4. Have the group make agreements that will allow the activity to be done safely.

5. Request that they make a serious commitment to each other to support their safety and well-being.

6. Once you reach the designated area, give the students their blindfolds. Ask them to decide who is going to be the leader. After five to seven minutes, call time and have the students remove their blindfolds. Give the teams a few minutes to talk about their experience of leading and being led. Then have the teams change leaders and continue the exercise.

7. After the second team's round of five to seven minutes, tell them to stop and remove their blindfolds. Once again, give them a few minutes to talk about their experiences. Have them acknowledge their teammates for guiding them and also for trusting them. Ask them to discuss the following question: If you were going to do this activity again, what changes would you make? Suggest that they discuss answers to this question with their teammates.

8. Bring the class together in a circle for closure. Have them take turns sharing what it felt like to be blindfolded and also what it felt like to be the leader. Hear are some possible discussion questions:

> "Did you feel fully comfortable and supported by your leader?"
>
> "If not, what could your leader have done differently to make you feel more trusting?"
>
> "What could you have done differently to make yourself feel more trusting of them?"
>
> "As the leader, how did it feel to have someone else depend on you? Did you feel worthy of the trust?"

61 Team Problem Solving

*P*roblems are the price you pay for progress.
—Branch Rickey

Purpose

When problems arise at school, it is often best to let students be part of the solution. This activity provides guidelines for arriving at win-win solutions through team problem solving.

Procedure

1. The concepts involved in this activity can be discussed with the class as a whole to set the stage for any particular problems that may arise.

2. Open the discussion in a manner similar to this: "What do all the following activities have in common?"

   > football games
   > baseball games
   > all professional sports
   > poker
   > Old Maid
   > all other card games (except solitaire)
   > most game shows
   > grading systems in schools (sometimes)
   > court cases
   > political elections
   > war

   Let the students respond. If they get it, congratulate them. If not, say, "Each of these activities has winners and losers. The fact is, many activities in life are set up as win–lose situations. To be a winner, it seems you have to defeat someone else. However, if you look at what makes a winning team, you notice that not only do they work together for a common goal, but they also care about each other. As each member grows in strength and ability, the entire team becomes more powerful. What this means is that there are no losers on a winning team. When problems arise, they are everybody's business. Solutions are found that allow each and every member to benefit. (Remember the lesson about their being no excess puzzle pieces in Activity 29,

"Everyone Belongs"?) You may be wondering if it is possible to have a game with no losers. Take a look and see."

3. Brainstorm typical problems that arise at school or discuss an actual problem that needs to be addressed. For example:

- Students in the playground got into a fight over which group can use the soccer ball.
- One group of students was picking on another group, making negative racial comments.
- On a cooperative learning science project, one of the students on the team is not doing his or her fair share of the work. Either other teammates will have to do extra work or the whole team's grade will suffer.

4. Distribute copies of the Team Problem Solving Worksheet and review this five step process with the class.

5. Now take one of the typical problems identified above or use the actual problem you want resolved, and practice using the five steps to arrive at a solution.

6. Next, have the students get into their Support Teams and work through one of the other problems using the ABCDE guidelines on the worksheet.

7. Have each Support Team report on its process and solution to the problem.

8. Indicate that this tool is available to them if problems arise in their own lives at school, at home, or at work.

**Team Problem Solving Worksheet:
Simple as ABCDE**

Agraee on what the problem is.
- What are the facts: Who, What, When, Where, How, and Why?

Brainstorm possible solutions.
- What do all interested parties want and need?

Choose the best solution.
- How could everyone's needs best be served?

Do it!
- Who will do what by when?

Evaluate and return to **A** if necessary.
- Is it working?
- Has the problem been solved?
- What more needs to happen?

62   The Three Blind Men and the Elephant

*N*othing that God ever made is the same thing
to more than one person.

—Zora Neale Hurston

Purpose

The purpose of this activity is for students to take greater ownership of their own viewpoint and to be more accepting of the points of view of others. It will help establish an important foundation for the next activity related to resolving conflicts.

Materials

Any object that has two different sides—a book that has a photograph on the front cover and a blank back cover, a T-shirt with an image on one side and nothing on the other, and so forth.

Procedure

1. Read the following story* to your students.

   > *Many years ago, there was a village where all of the citizens were blind. The older people told their children frightening stories about a monster who lived in the forest just outside of the village. Most people were afraid to enter the forest, for fear of being attacked by the ferocious beast.*
   >
   > *One day, three leaders of the city decided to go into the forest together and find out whether the stories were true. Together they ventured out, and eventually they located an elephant, who was grazing contentedly in a meadow.*
   >
   > *Now, the three men were blind, so they couldn't see the "monster." One of the blind men reached out and grasped the elephant's ear. Another groped around and felt the elephant's trunk. And the third took hold of one of the elephant's feet and legs. Armed with this information about the creature, they went back home.*

*This familiar story is adapted from *World Tales* by Idries Shah (New York: Harcourt Brace Jovanovich, 1979).

When they returned to the village, the three men called all the villagers around them. The townspeople were eager to hear a description of the creature that had inspired such fear. The first man, who had felt the elephant's ear, said, "I laid my hands on the creature, and I can tell you what it is. It is a large, rough thing, wide and broad, like a rug."

The second man, who had felt the elephant's trunk, broke in. "No," he cried, "I laid my hands on the creature, and I can tell you what it is. It is like a straight and hollow pipe, awful and destructive."

Then the third man, who touched the feet and legs, "Both of you are wrong. I laid my hands on the creature, and I can tell you what it is. It is mighty and firm like a pillar."

2. Now, stand in the middle of the class and hold up an object that has two different sides.

3. Ask one student who is sitting in a position to see only one side to describe what he or she sees.

4. Then ask a student who can only see the other side of the object to describe what it looks like from his or her viewpoint.

5. Repeat what each of the two students answered and ask the class who is right. When the students respond that both points of view are correct, ask how this is possible.

6. Explain that usually when people see things from different points of view, they assume that their perspective is right and therefore the other person must be wrong. This is the source of much conflict and fighting in the world. This demonstration makes it clear that it is possible for different people to have different points of view and that these can not only coexist but also enhance each person's total understanding of the situation.

7. This would serve as an excellent introduction to a multicultural lesson or discussion. You could select a historical event and consider it from various viewpoints. For example, what was the first Thanksgiving like for the children of the Pilgrims and for the Native Americans?

   The Civil War takes on an interesting perspective when viewed from the 186,000 African Americans who served—one-third of whom died—in the Union Army.

   It would be fascinating to consider what the California Gold Rush must have been like for the Chinese migrants who joined the "Forty-Niners."

   An excellent reference source is Ronald Takaki's *A Different Mirror: A History of Multicultural America* (Boston: Little, Brown, 1993).

8. This activity could also be used to help students understand how they can deal with their own personal conflicts in a nonviolent manner. The next exercise provides a structure for conflict management.

63 Let There Be Peace on Earth: Conflict Management*

We have grasped the mystery of the atom, and rejected the Sermon on the Mount. . . . The world has achieved brilliance without conscience. Ours is a world of nuclear giants and ethical infants. We know more about war than we do about peace, more about killing than we know about living.

—General Omar Bradley

People who fight fire with fire usually end up with ashes.

—Abigail Van Buren

Purpose

In situations where the students who are involved in a conflict are unable to resolve it themselves, this activity will let them get assistance from their Multicultural Support Team.

Procedure

1. The steps in the conflict management process are outlined on the following pages. Review these with your students first.

2. Then set up a series of demonstration role-plays involving two students in conflict and four students serving as conflict managers. Start with simple conflicts before engaging in more difficult issues. You may use one of these sample problem situations or decide on others:

   - Students in the playground got into a fight over which group would use the soccer ball.
   - One group of students was picking on another group, making negative racial comments.
   - On a cooperative learning science project, one of the students on the team is not doing his or her fair share of the work. Either other teammates will have to do extra work, or the whole team's grade will suffer.

*Adapted with permission from *Training High School Conflict Managers* (San Francisco: The Community Board Program, 1986).

3. Introduce the students to the process, step by step, allowing for any questions and observations as you go along.

4. Next, divide the class into their Support Teams and let them decide which two students will role-play the people who are in conflict and who will serve as conflict managers.

5. Select which conflict to use and have all groups working on the same one. Again, start with a simple conflict. Let them know that you are available as a resource if they need help.

6. When the groups are finished, bring them together for a class discussion. Find out how each group resolved the issue. Discuss the value of the process and how it can be used to resolve conflicts in the class, at school, at home, and in the community.

7. Continue with these small group role-plays over a period of days or weeks until everyone has had a turn and the skills of conflict management have been practiced to the point that students have integrated them. Gradually increase the severity of the conflict so that students are able to build upon earlier successes in applying conflict resolution skills to real-life situations.

> *I want you to feel like loving your opponent, and the way to do it is to give them the same credit for honesty of purpose which you would claim for yourself.*
> —Mohandas Gandhi

Conflict Management Worksheet
Step 1. Meet Separately

- Conflict managers meet separately with each person involved in the conflict.

- Introduce yourself.

- Describe the process and your role as conflict manager.

The purpose of this process is to help you resolve the conflict. The way it works is, first you will tell me what happened from your point of view. While we are doing this, the other person involved in this conflict is describing his or her perception of what happened to another conflict manager.

Then we will bring you both together and let you tell each other your side of the story, including your feelings about what happened. Once you understand each other's points of view better, we will explore possible solutions on which both of you can agree.

My role is to facilitate communication and to help you two settle this issue.

- Explain the agreements.

For this process to work, you must agree to the following:

1. *You are willing to use this process to resolve the conflict.*
2. *You will use appropriate language (no cursing or swearing).*
3. *You will behave appropriately (no threat of violence).*
4. *Everything that is said is confidential.*
5. *Conflict managers must report cases involving child abuse, pregnancy, and threats of serious violence.*

- Get their agreement to cooperate.

Do you agree to resolve the conflict by working with me through these five steps and by keeping these agreements?

- Ask the person now to explain what happened from his or her perspective to cause the conflict.

Step 2. Meet Together

- Bring the two parties together and review what was said to each of them separately. Confirm that each has agreed to resolve the conflict through this process.

- Explain that during this first part each person will have a chance to talk about the situation without interruption. He or she is to speak directly to you as the conflict manager, while the other person who is involved in the conflict gets to listen.

- Determine who will speak first, and ask this person to explain what happened from his or her perspective.

- Use effective listening skills (SHARE) to help clarify everyone's understanding of this person's experience.

- Summarize what you've heard, and confirm for accuracy.

- Acknowledge and validate: ``Thank you very much for describing your experience of this conflict. Given your perspective, I can appreciate how you feel.''

- Repeat this part of the process with the other person involved in the dispute.

- Summarize both points of view, emphasizing similarities.

Step 3. Build Mutual Understanding

- Determine who will speak first, and have this person communicate directly to the other person involved.

- Encourage this person to communicate responsibly, using ``I'' messages. (How I felt rather than what you did.)

- Allow feelings and emotions to be expressed.

- Ensure understanding, by having the other person restate what he or she heard.

- Summarize, validate, and acknowledge.

Step 4. Resolve the Conflict

- Ask each person how he or she would like to see the situation resolved.

- Explore possible solutions that would work for both people.

- Decide on a solution that is:
    —specific
    —realistic
    —mutually satisfactory.

- Schedule a follow-up session to take place within a week.

- Have each person sign an agreement to implement the solution and to be at the follow-up session.

- Acknowledge their willingness to resolve this issue.

Step 5. Follow-up on Results

- Welcome everyone back.

- Review the purpose of this meeting and the issues involved in the conflict management process.

- Ask each person to share what has happened since the last session.

- Invite them to discuss what they learned through this process.

- If the issue has been resolved, acknowledge their success.

- If the issue remains unresolved, discover what didn't work and repeat steps in the conflict management process until a new commitment is made.

63 Unequal Resources

In the beginning, our Creator gave all the races of mankind the same songs and the same drums to keep in touch with Him, to keep the faith. But people kept forgetting. In the fullness of time, the spiritual traditions of all the peoples—they are all the same—will be united again in a great gathering of their secret leaders. And they will gain power to remake the world.
—Mohawk prophecy as told by Tom Porter

Purpose

By now your students should be feeling comfortable within their Support Teams. This activity will challenge them to be concerned with others who are outside their own group.

As a model of the world where some groups have more resources—money, power, and so forth—than others, students will explore the human bias for competing rather than cooperating.

Materials

1. Scissors, ruler, paper clips, glue, black felt tip markers, and construction paper in six colors

2. Unequal Resources Task Sheet* for each group

3. Large envelopes to hold each group's resources. In the example below, the envelopes will contain the following resources as designated by group:

   - Group I: scissors, ruler, paper clips, pencils, and two 4" squares of red paper and two of white
   - Group II: scissors, glue and 8½" × 11" sheets of paper (two blue, two white, two gold)
   - Group III: felt-tipped markers and 8½" × 11" sheets of paper (two green, two white, two gold)
   - Group IV: 8½" × 11" sheets of paper (one each: green, gold, blue, red, and purple)

*Reprinted from J. W. Pfeiffer and J. E. Jones (Eds.), *The 1972 Annual Handbook for Group Facilitators*, (San Diego, CA: Pfeiffer & Company, 1972). Used with permission.

Procedure

1. Ask the students to get into their Support Teams and be seated at their individual tables. Distribute an envelope of materials and a Tasks Sheet to each group.

2. Tell the groups not to open their materials until you tell them to begin the task. Then explain that each group has different materials but that each group must complete the same tasks. Explain that they may bargain for the use of the materials and tools in any way that is mutually agreeable. Emphasize that the first group to complete all tasks is the winner.

3. Give the signal to begin and observe as much group process and bargaining behavior as you can, so that you can supply feedback later.

4. Stop the process when one or more of the teams have accurately completed the items described on the task sheet.

5. Complete the activity with a discussion of the process by asking for observations concerning allocation of resources, use of resources, teamwork within groups, willingness of people to share with other groups, bargaining efforts, tendencies to compete rather than cooperate, and so forth.

6. Draw analogies between this experiment and the experience of minority groups and people in underdeveloped nations. Enlist student suggestions for how the world could be made to work better.

Note: You may alter the complexity of the tasks and distribution of resources to fit the size of your class and age level of your students.

Unequal Resources Task Sheet

Each group is to complete the following tasks:

1. Make a 3″ × 3″ square of white paper.
2. Make a 4″ × 2″ rectangle of gold paper.
3. Make a four-link paper chain, each link in a different color.
4. Make a T-shaped piece 3″ × 5″ in green and white paper.
5. Make a 4″ × 4″ flag in any three colors.

The first group to complete all tasks is the winner. Groups may bargain with other groups for the use of materials and tools to complete the tasks on any mutually agreeable basis.

65 Streamers

One joy scatters a hundred griefs.

—Chinese Proverb

Purpose

The final activity in this section is meant to bring a sense of joy and celebration to the class as students thank one another for the positive ways in which everyone contributed.

Materials

Balls of yarn or crepe paper streamers, one roll per Multicultural Support Team; a different color for each team, preferably a color that is consistent with that team's colors.

Procedure

1. In order to have the students form a Circle of Friends that alternates members of each of the Support Teams, have the students within each team count from one to five. Ask all the "ones" to sit beside each other in the full circle, followed by the "twos," "threes," and so forth.

2. Let the students know that they are to say thank you to one of their teammates sitting in another part of the circle.
   They should be specific about what the other student did for which he or she is being thanked. For example:

   > "Thank you for helping me understand the math assignment."
   >
   > "Thank you for calling me at home to find out how I was feeling the time I was absent."
   >
   > "I appreciate your sense of humor."

3. Give all the "threes" a different color roll of crepe paper or ball of yarn. (See if you can match their team colors.) Instruct them to hold one end and gently toss the roll to the teammate that they are acknowledging.

4. After all the "threes" have said their thank you's and tossed their streamers, the students holding the rolls go next, in the same order as the rolls were received. Again they hold onto their part and toss the rest of the roll to the student they are acknowledging.
   Students should be told to pick students who have not yet been thanked and who are not holding a streamer.

5. Continue the process until everyone has said thank you and been thanked.

The process will create a web of streamers, representing the interconnectedness of all the students.

Chapter 7—Suggested Student Readings

Baylor, Byrd, & Peter Parnall. *The Other Way to Listen.* New York: Charles Scribner's Sons, 1978.

Beim and Beim. *Two Is a Team.* New York: Harcourt Brace, 1945.

Cecil, Laura. *Listen to This.* New York: Greenwillow, 1987.

Durrell, Anne, & Marilyn Sachs (Eds.). *The Big Book for Peace.* New York: Dutton, 1990.

Hazen, Nikki. *Grown-Ups Cry Too.* Carrboro, NC: Lollipop Power, 1973.

Mandelbaum, Phil. *You Be Me/I'll Be You.* Brooklyn, NY: Kane/Miller, 1990.

Paul, Paula. *You Can Hear a Magpie Smile.* New York: Nelson, 1980.

Ringgold, Faith. *Aunt Harriet's Underground Railroad in the Sky.* New York: Crown, 1992.

Shah, Idries. *World Tales.* New York: Harcourt Brace Jovanovich, 1979.

Chapter 8

Contribution
Celebrating Service

Any of us can dream, but seeking vision is always done not only to heal and fulfill one's own potential, but also to learn to use that potential to serve all our relations: the two-leggeds, the four-leggeds, the wingeds, those that crawl upon the Earth, and the Mother Earth herself.
—Brooke Medicine Eagle

Introduction

In the final analysis our most common basic link is that we all inhabit this small planet. We all breath the same air. We all cherish our children's future. And we are all mortal.
—John F. Kennedy

Chief Seattle was a peaceful and respected leader of the Native Americans of the Pacific Northwest over a hundred years ago. His people had been living on the land we now call America for thousands of years.

In the span of one single lifetime they had lost their land through bloody wars with white settlers from Europe. Exhausted and defeated, Chief Seattle's people were approached by representatives from the white man's government who wanted to buy their land.

"How can you buy the Sky? How can you own the rain and the wind?" was his response. Chief Seattle continued his impassioned plea by explaining his culture's sacred relationship with the earth.

"The earth does not belong to us. We belong to the earth."

The Chief's message is even more important now since it has been pretty much ignored over the past century.

He reminds us,

*"All things are connected like the blood that unites us. We did not weave the web of life, we are merely a strand in it. Whatever we do to the web, we do to ourselves."**

This final chapter extends the theme of Social Responsibility to a full global perspective. The activities encourage students to realize that their ultimate fulfillment will be found in service. Community-based and environmentally conscious projects are suggested.

The book ends on the theme of making the world a more peaceful and harmonious place for all.

> This is the confession of a half-educated man. My education prepared me superbly for a bird's-eye view of the world; it taught me how to recognize easily and instantly the things that differentiate one place or one people from another. But my education failed to teach me that the principal significance of such differences is that they are largely without significance. My education failed to grasp the fact that beyond the differences are realities scarcely comprehended because of their shattering simplicity. And the simplest reality of all is that the human community is one—greater than any of its parts, greater than the separateness imposed by actions, greater than the divergent faiths and allegiances or the depth and color of varying cultures.
>
> —Norman Cousins

Brother Eagle, Sister Sky, A Message from Chief Seattle, paintings by Susan Jeffers (New York: Dial, 1991).

66 Nobel Prize Winners

Winning the Prize (1963 Nobel Prize in physics) wasn't half as exciting as doing the work itself.
—Maria Gaeppert Mayer

Purpose

The purpose of this activity is to inspire children to dream of making a significant contribution to humanity.

The Nobel Prize, named after the Swedish industrialist Alfred Nobel who endowed the prize, is awarded for significant contributions in the areas of literature, economics, physics, chemistry, medicine and for efforts on behalf of world peace.

The Nobel Peace Prize has been awarded to men and women from various countries over the years. Among these are:

1992   Rigoberta Menchu
        Guatemalan Indian rights activist

1989   The Dalai Lama
        Exiled religious and political leader of Tibet

1984   Desmond Tutu
        South African Anglican Bishop and anti-apartheid activist

1979   Mother Teresa
        Missionary working with the sick and destitute of Calcutta

Procedure

1. Discuss the Nobel Peace Prize with your class.

   Share the contributions of past winners. If possible, use photos or film clips to enliven the presentation.

2. Have students do a report—written and/or oral—on a Nobel Prize winner of their choice. You may have them do individual projects or work in small teams on a cooperative learning project.

   Encourage students to be creative. Besides a standard report, suggest that they do a skit or play or use an interview format.

3. Provide time for students to present their reports.

4. Next have students think about the contributions they would like to make.

Imagine winning the Nobel Peace Prize 20 or 30 years from now. What would it be for? What would it say? For example, when the prize was awarded in 1992 the Nobel Committee said this about its recipient:

> *Rigoberta Menchu stands out as a vivid symbol of peace and reconciliation across ethnic cultural and social dividing lines, in her own country, on the American Continent and in the world.*

5. Have students work in pairs to develop their vision and wording for the award.

6. Have each student present the award to his or her partner in front of the whole class.

67 Lend a Hand

*The two kinds of people on earth that I mean
Are the people who lift and the people who lean.*
—Ella Wheeler Wilcox

Purpose

This activity* is meant to create a visual display of the power and beauty that comes from everyone lending a helping hand. It can also be used to promote good deeds at school, at home, and in the community.

Materials

a piece of white art paper (8″ square is a good size) for each student
pencils and other art supplies such as crayons, colored markers, stickers, magazines, glue and scissors, and so forth

Procedure

1. Distribute paper and art supplies, and ask students to trace an outline of their hand on the paper. Students can work in groups to help each other and share materials.

*This activity was suggested by a community service project held in San Francisco in December 1992 as a benefit for Project Open Hand, an organization that serves free meals to people with AIDS.

2. Next, invite students to decorate their hand drawing however they would like. For example:

   - Color it one color or many colors.
   - Draw a tattoo.
   - Draw jewelry.
   - Write or print their name on it as many times as will fit.
   - Write the names of the people who help them the most or that they would most like to help.

3. Now, have the students commit to lending a helping hand at school and home or in their community. After they have helped someone out, they can share how they lent a hand and at that point they can post their hand drawing on the wall.

   Students should hold onto their drawings until they have a chance to be helpful to someone—this being the price of admission in the "High Five Wall."

4. Create a "High Five Wall" by posting all the separate pages together to make one large mural.

68 Community-Service Projects

The contents of his (Sitting Bull's) pockets were often emptied into the hands of small, ragged little boys, nor could he understand how so much wealth should go brushing by, unmindful of the poor.

—Annie Oakley

Purpose

This activity helps students to become actively involved in contributing to their community.

Procedure

1. Brainstorm with your students about possible community service projects that your class or school might implement, such as:

   - A schoolwide canned food drive
   - An Adopt-a-Grandparent program at a local convalescent home

- Specific presentations and cookie making at a local preschool
- A schoolwide drive to collect toys for the local needy families in conjunction with other city groups
- A planned participation in the March of Dimes Mothers' Walk in March or April
- A car wash to raise funds for a local homeless shelter.

2. Help the group select one that they could realistically accomplish.

3. Consider whether academic credit for student involvement seems appropriate. If so, you might discuss with them what projects might provide the greatest opportunity to learn academic skills such as math (a fundraising event), English (a letter-writing campaign), history (a multicultural experience), physical sciences (an environmentally related project), social sciences (working with senior citizens or the underprivileged), and so on.

   Establish a way of documenting the learning—perhaps an independent study contract—in order to award credit for work done on the project.

4. Once the community service project has been selected, work with the students to identify the **purpose** of the project, the group's **goals** for the project, and the specific **actions** that will need to be taken to accomplish the project.

   For example:

   - The **purpose** of a canned food drive is to provide healthy food to people who might otherwise go hungry.
   - Our **goal** is to collect a total of 30 cans by the end of next week.
   - Some of the **actions** that we need to take are:

        —Brainstorm types of canned foods that are healthful and most useful (a good opportunity to learn about nutrition).

        —Identify possible agencies to which we could donate the cans.

        —Have each one of us be responsible for one can, either bringing it in ourselves or getting someone else to donate it, such as another teacher or a local merchant.

        —Find a place to store the cans until they are all received.

        —Find a way to deliver the cans to the agency we picked.

5. After the project is completed, hold a class meeting to discuss how it went.

   Possible discussion questions:

   "Did we accomplish our purpose?"
   "Did we achieve our goal?"
   "Was it easy or hard to do?"

"Did anything unexpected happen?"
"Was there anything that got in our way?"
"What did we learn from doing this?"
"How do you feel about what we did?"

If you are trying to transform a brutalized society into one where people can live in dignity and hope, you begin with the empowering of the most powerless. You build from the ground up.

—Adrienne Rich

69 Saving the Planet*

I had assumed that the Earth, the spirit of the Earth, noticed exceptions—those who wantonly damage it and those who do not. But the Earth is wise. It has given itself into the keeping of all, and all are therefore accountable.

—Alice Walker

The maltreatment of the natural world and its impoverishment leads to the impoverishment of the human soul. It is related to the outburst of violence in human society. To save the natural world today means to save what is human in humanity.

—Raisa M. Gorbachev

Purpose

Ecology is one area that involves all people of all cultures. Whether we are discussing the rain forests or recycling, oil spills or the ozone layer, environmental issues do not end neatly at the border of a particular country. We are indeed part of a global village.

The purpose of this activity is to instill in our children an awareness of their responsibility for the environment by starting a recycling program at their own school.

*The author wishes to acknowledge *50 SimpleThings Kids Can Do to Save the Earth* by Earth Works (Kansas City: Andrews and McNeal, 1990) for giving form to this idea and for a great book of 49 other ideas.

Procedure

1. Start with a discussion about the importance of recycling, focusing on the amount of paper, aluminum, and glass used at school.

2. Have students spend a day noticing and recording all the places in school where paper, aluminum and glass are used such as classrooms, cafeteria, offices, labs, and so forth.

3. Next discuss what would be involved in setting up a recycling center. Consider things such as:

   - A place to put containers to hold recycling materials
   - Containers—large, sturdy cardboard boxes or bins—to collect paper, metal, and glass.
   - Signs to label containers.
   - Transportation to a recycling center or out on the sidewalk if curbside pickup is available in your area.

4. Once the recycling center is set up, how will everyone know about it and be encouraged to use it? Brainstorm with your students how to get the whole school involved. Perhaps:

   - Posters
   - In-school announcements
   - Contests
   - Article in school newspaper
   - Press releases to local newspaper, radio, and TV stations

70 World Travelers

Certainly, travel is more than the seeing of sights; it is a change that goes on, deep and permanent, in the ideas of living.

—Miriam Beard

Purpose

Through this activity, students get to imagine traveling around the world—visiting places they have always wanted to see, returning to their ancestral homeland, or exploring an exotic locale with a totally different culture.

Their appreciation for people and customs of different cultures will be enhanced.

Procedure

1. Engage the students in a discussion of various countries and cultures around the world. Find out what places your students have already visited. Have them consider what part of the world they would like to see and what they have heard about these places. Using a large map to help students locate the various destinations would help expand their sights.

2. Have students work together in their Support Teams or cooperative learning group to plan an itinerary of places their groups wants to visit on their world tour.

3. Establish learning centers at various places around the room and ask each team to be responsible for setting up a display of materials related to one of the cities or countries that they are planning to visit. Coordinate the process so that each team is researching a different location. Suggest to the students that they go to a travel agency to get posters and brochures on their destination. Have them use their geography books, encyclopedia, or other books from the library to learn about this country, its people, language, culture, customs, money system, and so forth.

   Brainstorm with your students other things they could include in their display, such as:

   - articles of clothing
   - stamps
   - magazines, newspapers
   - photographs
   - food
   - arts and crafts

4. When the projects are completed, allow class time for the student teams to report on their trip, highlighting the destination on display. Let the students roam around to each of the learning centers.

5. This could be developed into an entire unit with academic credit being given for the subject areas that the students learned about through their involvement in the project.

71 Pen Pals

*Why is it that you can sometimes feel the reality of
people more keenly through a letter than face to face?*
—Anne Morrow Lindbergh

Purpose

For students to realize that in countries around the world there are children
just like themselves with similar feelings, wants, and needs.

This will help to humanize "foreigners" and build more respect for
people from different cultures.

Procedure

1. One good way of introducing this activity is to read the book *A Country
   Far Away* by Nigel Gray and Philippe Dupasqui (New York: Orchard
   Books, 1991).

   It is a delightful story of two young boys—one African and one
   American—with one text and two sets of illustrations showing the
   same actions in two very different cultures. The book ends with each
   child imagining that he will visit the other's country and make a friend.

2. Ask the students to think about a country that they would like to visit
   and perhaps make a friend.

   Since they are going to communicate in writing, they should consider possible difficulties with language and ways with which they will
   deal with this. You might limit the activity to countries where people
   speak the same language as the student or find a source for translators.

3. Next, the students will need to find a way to connect with children in
   the desired countries. One possibility is to call or write to an organization that works in this area such as:

   > World Pen Pals
   > 1690 Como Avenue
   > St. Paul, MN 55108
   > (612) 647-0191

   World Pen Pals lists more than 40,000 names of people worldwide who
   are looking for pen pals.

Two other organizations that will line up pen pals are:

Worldwide Friendship International
3749 Brice Run Road, Suite A
Randallstown, MD 21133

For Our Children's Sake
475 Riverside Drive, Suite 828
New York, NY 10115
(Send self-addressed stamped envelope.)

4. Have students write their letter to their pen pal and share it in their Support Team before sending it. Support Team members could offer feedback and suggestions, and you could help with spelling and so forth as needed.

5. As the letters from the Pen Pals in various parts of the world begin to be received by the students, allow them to share these and post them for others to read.

72 A World of Friends*

*To him in whom love dwells,
the whole world is but one family.*

—Buddha

Purpose

The local chapter of the American Red Cross will provide you with twenty-five empty boxes which, when filled, they will send to a country you choose. For information write:

American Red Cross, National Headquarters
International/Youth Services
Attention: Friendship Boxes
Washington, DC 20006

This is an enjoyable way for your students to connect with children in other parts of the world. You may want to start with needy children in your own neighborhood, city, state, or other parts of the United States.

*This activity was suggested by an excellent book of projects for "kids who want to help people, animals and the world we live in," *The Helping Hands Handbook* by Patricia Adams and Jean Marzollo (New York: Random House, 1992).

Procedure

1. Discuss with your students the idea of sending boxes of gifts to needy children throughout the world. Consider:

   "Is this something you would like to do?"

   "What kinds of things would we send?"

   "What kinds of things would you like to receive if it were being sent to you?"

   "To what countries would we consider sending gifts?"

   "What do we know about conditions in these countries?"

   "If you were a child in this country what would you like to get from children in the United States?"

   As the discussion proceeds, develop a list of items that might be put in these boxes such as soap, combs, marbles, photographs, arts and crafts, and so forth.

2. You may want to contact the Red Cross yourself to get all the necessary information and request the boxes, or you may want to include students in this process. Students could brainstorm their questions and help draft the letter.

3. With your students, decide if each student will fill a box or if they will work in teams.

4. Provide a place in the classroom for the items that are collected to be stored until the boxes are filled and sent.

5. Class time could be used to make items such as bookmarks, greeting cards, and so forth.

73 World Leaders

Why do we need leaders in a free country? I would answer that the leader's function is to determine, in any crisis, which of our possible selves will act.
—Lyman Bryson

Purpose

As the next generation of world citizens, our children have a stake in the future and how today's leaders are impacting that future.

This activity helps students create a vision of the world in which they want to live and how they might be able to influence that future.

Procedure

1. Brainstorm with your students all the world leaders they are able to name. They may need to do some research to add names to those that they know.

2. Ask the students to imagine that these world leaders will be gathered for a conference on the future and that the students will have a chance to present to these leaders. The topic of the presentation is "the world we want and what we need to do about it now."

3. Hand out the worksheet, The World We Want, and invite the students to use this as a way of structuring their thoughts.

4. Let the students work with their Support Teams or in a cooperative learning group to prepare and practice their presentations.

5. Schedule a Future of the World Conference at which students will present their vision and suggestions. You may want to invite some guests to serve as the panel of world leaders. These guests could include other teachers or administrators, parents, local business people or community leaders, or older students.

6. Have each team of students do their presentations.

7. Afterwards, bring the students together into a class circle and discuss how the conference went.

    Possible discussion questions are as follows:

    "How do you feel about the conference?"

    "What did you like about the presentations?"

"Were there common themes from the different presentations?"

"Did you say what you wanted to the world leaders?"

"Is there anything you would do differently if you really had the opportunity to be present at such a conference?"

The World We Want Worksheet

1. My **vision** of a better world is:

   _____

   _____

   _____

2. A better world would have **more**:

   _____

   _____

   _____

3. A better world would have **less**:

   _____

   _____

   _____

4. In a better world **all people** would:

   _____

   _____

   _____

5. If I were a **world leader** I would:

   _____

   _____

   _____

6. **All of us** must work together to:

   _____

   _____

   _____

74 World Leaders: The Televised Summit

*W*hat the best and wisest parent wants for his own child
that must be what the community wants for all its
children.

—John Dewey

Purpose

This final video recording activity will give your students an opportunity to
internalize the lessons learned about social responsibility.

Materials

Video camera or camcorder, VCR playback equipment, TV monitor and
blank video tape.

Procedure

Structured Approach
Use the previous activity, "World Leaders," and record it as if it were a
satellite program being simultaneously broadcast around the world.

Creative Approach
As with the previous video activities (Activities 17 and 33), use the worksheet Part IV—Key Learnings to select a topic, decide on a format for the TV
show, and let students run with it.

75 I'd Like to Teach the World to Sing

What good is music? None . . . and that is the point. To the world and its states and armies and factories and Leaders, music says, "You are irrelevant"; and arrogant and gentle as a god, to the suffering man it says only "Listen." For being saved is not the point. Music saves nothing. Merciful, uncaring, it denies and breaks down all the shelters, the houses men build for themselves, that they may see the sky.

—Ursula K. Le Guin

While I listened, music was to my soul what the atmosphere is to my body; it was the breath of my inward life. I felt, more deeply than ever, that music is the highest symbol of the infinite and holy.

—Lydia Maria Child

Purpose

For many of us, music has a healing effect. Music can transcend time and place and can unite people in "perfect harmony."

This activity is meant to be an uplifting celebration of humanity in all its wonderful diversity.

Procedure

1. With your students, select a song, such as, "I'd Like to Teach the World to Sing in Perfect Harmony," that is uplifting and has an easy melody.

2. Get help from students, parents, other teachers and community members to translate the lyrics of this song into all the languages spoken by your students so that all cultures are included. You may also want to include any additional languages that are important to your students.

3. Teach yourself how to sing the song in each of the different languages.

4. Plan a time when you can have a fiesta—a day to *celebrate diversity.* Brainstorm with your students whom they would like to invite:

   • Just their class
   • One or a few other classes

- The entire school
- Other schools
- Their families
- Other community members

Decide what kinds of activities they would like to plan for the day:

- Multicultural food fair
- Art and crafts
- Dance and music
- Showing their TV programs
- Doing other activities from the book
- A sing-along, in the many languages of our cultures, "in perfect harmony."

Part IV—Key Learnings Worksheet

I listen
carefully to hear
what the other person
means.

I look for
peaceful
solutions
to conflict.

I allow others
to have their
own point of view
even if it is
different from mine.

I know that
I can and do
make a difference

I am able
to work as part of
a team.

I feel good about
myself when I
am serving others
who are less
fortunate.

I am
trustworthy.

I am responsible
for taking good
care of the planet.

I am
able to
solve problems.

I envision
a better world
where people
take care of
each other.

Part IV—Teacher Checklist:
Turning Problems into Opportunities for Learning

❏ Have I come to appreciate that I am probably not going to change the world overnight, and that building esteem for oneself and others is ongoing process?

❏ Am I observing what's working as well as what's not working in a nonjudgmental way so that I can learn from the experience and constantly improve?

❏ Have I been encouraging my students to be open-minded and accepting of ``failures'' as steps on the road to success?

❏ When incidents of stereotyping, prejudice, and discrimination occur, have I developed the skills to turn these into learning opportunities for the students involved?

❏ Am I able to stay calm and objective rather than react in an emotional way so that I can maintain the role of coach in helping students deal with these situations?

❏ Have I learned how to coach students who have been on the receiving end of ethnic slurs or other types of put-downs in a way that empowers them rather than promotes feelings of either victimization or revenge?

❏ Have I learned how to coach students who were the perpetrators of ethnic slurs or other types of put-downs so that they develop greater sensitivity, increase their awareness, and act differently in the future?

❏ Do we hold regular class meetings so that students can discuss their feelings and solve their own problems?

Chapter 8—Suggested Student Readings

Adams, Patricia, & Jean Marzollo. *The Helping Hands Handbook.* New York: Random House, 1992.

Coer, Eleanor B. *Sadako and the Thousand Paper Cranes.* New York: Macmillan, 1979.

Earthworks Group. *50 Simple Things Kids Can Do to Save the Earth.* Kansas City: Andrews and McMeel, 1990.

Gray, Niget, & Philippe Dupasquies. *A Country Far Away.* New York: Orchard Books, 1988.

Jeffers, Susan. *Brother Eagle, Sister Sky: A Message from Chief Seattle.* New York: Dial, 1991.

Peretz, I. C. *The Case Against the Wind and Other Stories,* translated and adapted by Esther Hautzig. New York: Macmillan, 1975.

References and Resources

References

Banks, James A. *Teaching Strategies for Ethnic Studies, 5th ed.* Boston: Allyn and Bacon, 1991.
———. *Multiethnic Education: Theory and Practice, 2nd ed.* Boston: Allyn and Bacon, 1988.

Banks, James A., & Cherry A. McGee Banks (Eds). *Multicultural Education: Issues and Perspectives.* Boston: Allyn and Bacon, 1989.

Board of Education of the City of New York. *Children of the Rainbow.* New York: Department of Education, 1991.

Bourdieu, Pierre. "The Forms of Capital." In *Handbook of Theory and Research for the Sociology of Education,* edited by John G. Richardson. New York: Greenwood Press, 1986.

Branden, Nathaniel. *The Power of Self-Esteem.* Deerfield Beach, FL: Health Communications, 1992.

Canfield, Jack, & Frank Siccone. *101 Ways to Develop Students' Self-Esteem and Responsibility, Volumes I and II.* Boston: Allyn and Bacon, 1993.

Cleveland Public Schools. *Pupil Adjustment in a Desegregated Setting.* Cleveland: Cleveland Public Schools, 1978.

Community Board Programs. *Training High School Conflict Managers.* San Francisco, CA, 1986.

Dunham, Carrol, et al. *Mamatoto: A Celebration of Birth.* New York: Penguin Books, 1991.

Cummins, Jim. *Empowering Minority Students.* Sacramento: California Association for Bilingual Education, 1989.

Larrivee, Barbara. *Strategies for Effective Classroom Management.* Boston: Allyn and Bacon, 1992.

Lazear, David. *Seven Ways of Teaching.* Palatine, IL: Skylight Publishing, 1991.

Matiella, Ana Consuelo. *Positively Different.* Santa Cruz, CA: Network Publication, 1991.

Nieto, Sonia. *Affirming Diversity: The Sociopolitical Context of Multicultural Education.* New York: Longman, 1992.

Pfieffer, J. William, & John E. Jones, (Eds.), *The 1972 Annual Handbook for Group Facilitators.* San Diego, University Associates, 1972.

Shaftel, Fannie R., & George Shaftel. *Role-Playing in the Curriculum, 2nd ed.* Engelwood Cliffs, NJ: Prentice-Hall, 1982.

Takaki, Ronald. *A Different Mirror: A History of Multicultural America.* Boston: Little, Brown, 1993.

Tiedt, Pamela L., & Iris M. Tiedt. *Multicultural Teaching, 3rd ed.* Boston: Allyn and Bacon, 1990.

Suggested Readings

Teacher Resources— Multicultural

Abbey, Nancy, Claire Brindis, & Manual Casas. *Family Life Education in Multicultural Classrooms: Practical Guidelines.* Santa Cruz, CA: ETR Associates/Network Publications, 1990.

Albert, R. D. *The intercultural sensitizer or culture assimilator: A cognitive approach.* In D. Landis & R. W. Brislin (Eds.), *Handbook of Intercultural Training* (Vol. 2). New York: Pergamon Press, 1983.

Allen, Judy, Earldene McNeill, & Velma Schmidt. *Cultural Awareness for Children.* Menlo Park, CA: Addison-Wesley, 1992.

Allport, Gordon W. *The Nature of Prejudice.* Reading, MA: Addison-Wesley, 1979.

Appleton, Nicholas. *Cultural Pluralism in Education: Theoretical Foundations.* New York: Longman, 1983.

Austin, Mary C. *Promoting World Understanding Through Literature, K–8.* Littleton, CO: Libraries Unlimited, 1983.

Baker, Gwendolyn C. *Planning and Organizing for Multicultural Instruction.* Reading, MA: Addison-Wesley, 1983.

Ball, L., et al. *Kaleidoscope.* Elizabethtown, PA: Continental Press, 1988.

Belotti, Elena Gianini. *What Are Little Girls Made Of?* New York: Schocken Books, 1976.

Bennett, Christine. *Comprehensive Multicultural Education: Theory and Practice, 2nd ed.* Boston: Allyn and Bacon, 1990.

Boyer, James. *Multicultural Education: Product and Process.* Manhattan, KS: Urban Education Center, 1985.

Brislin, R. W., K. Cushner, C. Cherrie, & M. Young. *Intercultural Interactions: A Practical Guide.* Newbury Park, CA: Sage Publications, 1986.

Brislin, R., & P. Pedersen. *Cross-Cultural Orientation Programs.* New York: Gardner Press, 1976.

Caballero, Jane, & Derek Whordley. *New Children Around the World.* Atlanta, GA: Humanics Limited, 1990.

California State Department of Education, Office of Intergroup Relations. *Guide for Multicultural Education Content and Context.* Sacramento: California Department of Education, 1977.

California State Department of Education. *Recommended Readings in Literature: Kindergarten Through Grade Eight.* Sacramento: California State Department of Education, 1988.

Carlson, Dale. *Girls Are Equal Too.* Forge Village, MA: Harcourt Brace Jovanovich, 1973.

Carmichael, Carrie. *Nonsexist Child Raising.* Boston: Beacon Press, 1977.

Cheek, Helen M. *Handbook for Conducting Equity Activities in Mathematics Education.* Reston, VA: National Council of Teachers of Mathematics, 1984.

Children's Creative Response to Conflict Program Staff. *The Friendly Classroom for a Small Planet.* Philadelphia: New Society Publishers, 1988.

Colgin, Mary Lou. *Chants for Children.* New York: Colgin Publishing, 1982.

Combs, Arthur. *A Personal Approach to Teaching: Beliefs That Make a Difference.* Boston: Allyn and Bacon, 1982.

Council on Interracial Books for Children. *Guidelines for Selecting Bias-Free Textbooks and Storybooks.* New York: Council on Interracial Books for Children.

———. *Stereotypes, Distortions and Omissions in U.S. History Textbooks.* New York: Council on Interracial Books for Children.

Cuban, L. The at-risk label and the problem of urban school reform. *Phi Delta Kappan*, 10(70), 780–784, 799–801, 1989.

Davis, G., & M. Thomas. *Effective Schools and Effective Teachers.* Boston: Allyn and Bacon, 1989.

Derman-Sparks, Louise. *Anti-Bias Curriculum.* Washington, DC: National Association for the Education of Young Children, 1990.

Diagram Group. *The Way to Play.* New York: Paddington Press Ltd, 1975.

Edmonds, Ann C. *Our Global Village: Japan.* St. Louis, MO: Milliken, 1990.

Fenstermacher, G. D., & J. F. Soltis. *Approaches to Teaching.* New York: Teachers College Press, 1986.

Fleming, Bonnie, et al. *Resources for Creative Teaching in Early Childhood Education.* New York: Harcourt Brace Jovanovich, 1972.

Fradd, S., & M. J. Weismantel. *Meeting the Needs of Culturally and Linguistically Different Students: A Handbook for Educators.* Boston: College-Hill, 1989.

Garcia, Ricardo L. *Education for Cultural Pluralism: Global Roots Stew.* Bloomington, IN: Phi Delta Kappa Educational Foundation, 1981.

Gollnick, Donna M., & Phillip C. Chinn. *Multicultural Education in a Pluralistic Society, 3rd ed.* Columbus, OH: Merrill, 1990.

Grant, Carl, & Christine Sleeter. *Turning on Learning: Five Approaches for Multicultural Teaching Plans for Race, Class, Gender, and Disability.* Columbus, OH: Merrill, 1989.

Griber, Barbara, & Sue Griber. *Learning about Our Country.* Palos Verdes, CA: Frank Schaffer, 1990.

Grossman, H. *Educating Hispanic Students: Cultural Implications for Instruction, Classroom Management, Counseling, and Assessment.* Springfield, IL: Charles C Thomas, 1984.

————. *Trouble-Free Teaching: Solutions to Behavior Problems in the Classroom.* Mountain View, CA: Mayfield, 1990.

Grunfeld, Frederic. *Games of the World.* New York: Holt, 1975.

Hernandez, Hilda. *Multicultural Education.* Columbus, OH: Merrill, 1989.

Jersin, P. D. What is your educational philosophy? *Clearing House,* 46, 274–278, 1972.

Juffer, K.A. *Culture Shock: A Theoretical Framework for Understanding Adaptation.* In J. Bradsford (Ed.), Monograph Series: BUENO Center for Multicultural Education, 4, 136–149, 1983.

Kamp, Susan H., & Philip C. Chinn. *A Multiethnic Curriculum for Special Education Students.* Reston, VA: Council for Exceptional Children, 1982.

Kendall, Frances E. *Diversity in the Classroom.* New York: Teachers College Press, 1983.

Klawitter, Pamela. *Learning about Communities.* St. Louis, MO: Milliken, 1985.

Klepper, Nancy. *Our Global Village: Africa.* St. Louis, MO: Milliken, 1990.

————. *Our Global Village: Mexico.* St. Louis, MO: Milliken, 1990.

Kruse, Ginny M. *Multicultural Children's and Young Adult Literature.* Madison: University of Wisconsin, Cooperative Children's Book Center, 1989.

Lee, Nancy, & Linda Oldham. *Hands-on Heritage.* Long Beach, CA: Hands-on Publications, 1978.

Levine, Deena. *The Cultural Puzzle: Cross-Cultural Communications for English as a Second Language.* Englewood Cliffs, NJ: Prentice-Hall, 1987.

Lipson, Greta Barclay, & Jane A. Romatowski. *Ethnic Pride.* Carthage, IL: Good Apple, 1983.

Lynch, J. *Multicultural Education in a Global Society.* London: Falmer Press, 1989.

McKinnon, Elizabeth. *Special Day Celebration.* Everett, WA: Warren, 1989.

Moser, Sharon J. *Children in the U.S.A.* St. Louis, MO: Milliken, 1982.

National Information Center for Children and Youth with Handicaps. *Minority Issues in Special Education: A Portrait of the Future.* Washington, DC: Author, 1988.

Ohanesian, Anne Marie. *Social Studies Mini-Units.* Grand Rapids, MI: Instructional Fair, 1991.

Ortiz, Alba A., & Bruce A. Ramirez. *Schools and the Culturally Diverse Exceptional Student: Promising Practices and Future Directions.* Reston, VA: Council for Exceptional Children, 1989.

Pasternak, Michael G. *Helping Kids Learn Multi-Cultural Concepts.* Champaign, IL: Research Press, 1979.

Pedersen, Paul. *A Handbook for Developing Multicultural Awareness.* Alexandria, VA: American Association for Counseling and Development, 1988.

Phinney, Jean S., & Mary Jane Rotheram (Eds.). *Children's Ethnic Socialization.* Newbury Park, CA: Sage Publications, 1987.

Pine, G. J., & A. G. Hillard. Rx for racism: Imperatives for American's schools. *Phi Delta Kappan,* 71(8), 593-600, 1990.

Ramsey, Patricia G. *Teaching and Learning in a Diverse World: Multicultural Education for Young Children.* New York: Teachers College Press, Columbia University, 1987.

Schubert, Barbara, & Marlene Bird. *Annese.* Reflections Images, 1976.

————. *Black History.* Reflections Images, 1977.

————. *Holiday Customs Around the World.* Reflections Images, 1977.

————. *Japanese.* Reflections Images, 1985.

————. *Mexicans.* Reflections Images, 1976.

Seaman, Rosie. *Discovering Ourselves.* Belmont, CA: David S. Lake, 1987.

———. *Discovering Our World.* Belmont, CA: David S. Lake, 1987.

Sleeter, Christine E. *Empowerment Through Multicultural Education.* Albany, NY: SUNY Press, 1991.

———. *Keepers of the American Dream: A Study of Staff Development and Multicultural Education.* London: Falmer Press, 1992.

Sleeter, C. E., & C. A. Grant. *Making Choices for Multicultural Education: Five Approaches to Race, Class, and Gender.* Columbus, OH: Merrill, 1988.

Spolsky, Bernard. *Language and Education in Multilingual Settings.* San Diego, CA: College-Hill Press, 1989.

Stacey, York. *Roots and Wings.* St. Paul, MN: Toys'n Things Press, 1991.

Stacy, Judith. *And Jill Came Tumbling After: Sexism in American Education.* New York: Dell, 1974.

Thomas, Donald. *Pluralism Gone Mad.* Bloomington, IN: Phi Delta Kappa Educational Foundation, 1981.

Tiedt, Pamela M., & Iris McClellan, et al. *Reading/ Thinking/Writing: A Holistic Language and Literacy Program for the K–8 Classroom.* Boston: Allyn and Bacon, 1989.

Trueba, Henry T. *Raising Silent Voices: Educating the Linguistic Minorities for the 21st Century.* New York: Newbury House Publishers, 1989.

Vargas, Roberto, & Samuel Martinez. *Razalogia: Community Learning for a New Society.* Oakland, CA: Razagenta Associates, 1984.

Warren, Jean, & Elizabeth McKinnon. *Small World Celebrations.* Everett, WA: Warren, 1988.

Williams, Leslie, & Yvonne DeGactone. *Alerta.* Reading, MA: Addison-Wesley, 1985.

Teacher Resources— Self-Esteem

Bean, Reynold, & Harris Clemes. *The Four Conditions of Self-Esteem.* Santa Cruz, CA: ETR Associates/Network Publications, 1977. Revised 1992.

Borba, Michele. *Esteem Builders: A K–8 Self-Esteem Curriculum for Improving Students' Achievement, Behavior and School Climate.* Rolling Hills Estates, CA: Jalmar Press, 1989.

Canfield, Jack, & Harold Wells. *100 Ways to Enhance Self-Concept in the Classroom.* Englewood Cliffs, NJ: Prentice-Hall, 1976.

Canfield, Jack, et al. *Self-Esteem in the Classroom: A Curriculum Guide.* Self-Esteem Seminars, 6035 Bristol Parkway, Culver City, CA 90230, 1986, 1990.

Durfee, Cliff. *More Teachable Moments.* San Diego, CA: Live, Love, Laugh, 1983.

McCarty, Hanoch. *Self-Esteem: The Bottom Line in School Success.* Galt, CA: Hanoch McCarty & Association, 1992.

Moorman, Chick, & Dee Dishon. *Our Classroom: We Can Learn Together.* Englewood Cliffs, NJ: Prentice-Hall, 1983.

Palomares, Uvaldo, et al. *The Human Development Program.* Spring Valley, CA: Magic Circle, 1970.

Reasoner, Robert. *Building Self-Esteem.* Palo Alto, CA: Consulting Psychologists Press, 1982.

Siccone, Frank. *Responsibility: The Most Basic "R."* San Francisco: Siccone Institute, 1987.

———. *Teacher as Coach.* San Francisco: Siccone Institute, 1988.

———. (Ed.). *The Best of Self-Esteem.* San Francisco: Siccone Institute, 1990.

Children's Books—African American

Aardema, Verna. *Behind the Back of the Mountain.* New York: Dial, 1973.

———. *Bimwili & the Zimibi; A Tale from Zanzibar.* New York: Dial, 1985.

———. *Black Folktales from Southern Africa.* New York: Dial, 1973.

———. *Bringing the Rain to Kapiti Plain.* New York: Dial, 1981.

———. *Half-a-Ball-of-Kenki; An Ashanti Tale.* New York: Warner, 1979.

———. *Oh Kojo! How Could You.* New York: Dial, 1984.

———. *Tales from Story Hat.* New York: Coward, 1960.

———. *What's So Funny, Ketu?* New York: Dial, 1982.

———. *Who's in the Rabbit House? A Masai Tale.* New York: Dial, 1977.

————. *Why Mosquitoes Buzz in People's Ears*. New York: Dial, 1975.

Adler, C. S. *Always and Forever Friends*. New York: Clarion, 1988.

Adoff, Arnold. *All the Colors of the Races*. New York: Lothrop, 1982.

————. *Black Is Brown Is Tan*. New York: Harper & Row, 1973.

Aliki. *A Week Is a Flower: The Life of George Washington Carver*. New York: Prentice-Hall, 1965.

Arkhurst, Joyce. *The Adventures of Spider: West African Tales*. New York: Little, Brown, 1964.

Bang, Molly. *Ten, Nine, Eight*. New York: Greenwillow, 1983.

————. *Two Is a Team*. New York: Harcourt, Brace, 1945.

Boone-Jones. *Martin Luther King, Jr.: A Picture Story*. Chicago: Children's Press, 1968.

Brenner, Barbara. *Wagon Wheels*. New York: Harper & Row, 1978.

Brooks, Gwendolyn. *Bronzeville Boys and Girls*. New York: Harper & Row, 1956.

Bunin, S, & Bunin, C. *Is That Your Sister?* New York: Pantheon, 1976.

Caines, Jeanette. *Abby*. New York: Harper & Row, 1984.

————. *Daddy*. New York: Harper & Row, 1977.

————. *Just Us Women*. New York: Harper & Row, 1982.

Cameron, Ann. *More Stories Julian Tells*. New York: Knopf, 1986.

————. *The Stories Julian Tells*. New York: Pantheon, 1981.

Clark, Mollie. *Congo Boy*. New York: Scholastic, 1971.

Clayton, Edward. *Martin Luther King: The Peaceful Warrior*. New York: Archway, 1989.

Clifton, Lucille. *Amifka*. New York: Dutton, 1973.

————. *Don't You Remember?* New York: Dutton, 1973.

————. *Everett Anderson's Friend*. New York: Holt, 1976.

————. *Everett Anderson's Goodbye*. New York: Holt, 1976.

————. *Everett Anderson's Nine Month Long*. New York: Holt, 1978.

————. *My Friend Jacob*. New York: Dutton, 1980.

————. *Some of the Days of Everett Anderson*. New York: Holt.

————. *The Black BC's*. New York: Dutton, 1970.

————. *The Boy Who Didn't Believe in Spring*. New York: Dutton, 1973.

————. *The Lucky Stone*. New York: Delacorte, 1979.

————. *Three Wishes*. New York: Viking, 1976.

Cohen, Barbara. *Thank You, Jackie Robinson*. New York: Lothrop, Lee & Shepard, a division of William Morrow, 1988.

Courlander, Harold. *The Crest and the Hide and Other African Stories*. New York: Putnam Publishing Group, 1982.

Cummings, Pat. *Jimmy Lee Did It*. New York: Lothrop, 1985.

Daly, Nikki. *Not So Fast Songololo*. New York: Puffin, 1985.

Dobrin, Arnold. *Josephine's Magination*. New York: Scholastic, 1975.

Feelings, Muriel. *Jambo Means Hello*. New York: Dial, 1974.

————. *Moja Means One: Swahili Counting Book*. New York: Dial, 1971.

Feelings, Tom. *Black Pilgrimage*. New York: Lothrop, 1972.

Felton, Harold. *John Henry and His Hammer*. New York: Knopf, 1950.

Fox, Paula. *Slave Dancer*, New York: Bradbury Press, Macmillan, 1973.

Freeman, Don. *Corduroy*. New York: Viking. 1965.

————. *A Pocket for Corduroy*. New York: Viking, 1967.

Giovanni, Nikki. *Spin a Soft Black Song*. New York: Hill & Wang, 1971.

Greene, Bette. *Philip Hall Likes Me, I Reckon Maybe*. New York: Dell, 1975.

Greenfield, Eloise. *Daydreamers*. New York: Dial, 1981.

————. *Honey, I Love and Other Love Poems*. New York: Crowel, 1978.

————. *Me and Nessie*. New York: Crowell, 1975.

————. *Childtimes: A Three Generation Memoir*. New York: Crowell, 1979.

————. *Mary McLeod Bethune*. New York: Crowell, 1979.

————. *Nathaniel Talking*. New York: Black Butterfly Children's Books, 1988.

————. *Paul Robeson*. New York: Crowell, 1975.

————. *Rosa Parks*. New York: Crowell, 1973.

————. *She Come Bringing Me That Little Baby Girl*. Philadelphia: Lippincott, 1974.

———. *Sister.* New York: Crowell, 1974.

———. *Talk about a Family.* New York: Lippincott, 1978.

Grifalconi, Ann. *The Village of Round and Square Houses.* Boston: Little, Brown, 1980.

Grimes, Nikki. *Something on My Mind.* New York: Dial, 1978.

Hamilton, Virginia. *House of Dies Drear.* New York: Macmillan, 1968.

———. *Drylongso.* New York: Harcourt Brace Jovanovich, 1993.

Havill, Juanita. *Jamaica's Find.* Boston: Houghton Mifflin, 1986.

Hayes, Sarah. *Clap Your Hands.* New York: Lothrop, 1988.

———. *Eat Up, Gemma.* New York: Lothrop. 1988.

———. *Happy Christmas Gemma.* New York: Lothrop, 1986.

Hessey, Anne. *Giant Treasury of Brer Rabbit.* New York: Outlet, 1991.

Hill, Elizabeth. *Evan's Corner.* New York: Holt, 1967.

Isadora, Rachel. *Babies.* New York: Greenwillow, 1990.

———. *Ben's Trumpet.* New York: Greenwillow, 1979.

———. *City Seen from A to Z.* New York: Greenwillow, 1983.

———. *Friends.* New York: Greenwillow, 1990.

Jones, Bessie, & Bess Lomax Howes. *Step Is Down: Games, Plays, Songs Stories from the Afro-American Heritage.* Athens: University of Georgia, 1984.

Joseph, Lynn. *Coconut Kind of Day/Island Poems.* New York: Lothrop, 1990.

Keats, Ezra Jack. *A Letter to Amy.* New York: Harper & Row, 1968.

———. *John Henry.* New York: Pantheon, 1965.

———. *Peter's Chair.* New York: Harper & Row, 1967.

———. *The Snowy Day.* New York: Viking, 1962.

———. *Whistle for Willie.* New York: Viking, 1965.

Keats, Erza Jack, & Pat Cherr. *My Dog Is Lost.* New York: Harper & Row, 1960.

Knutson, Barbara. *How the Guinea Fowl Got Her Spots.* Minneapolis, MN: Carolrhoda, 1990.

———. *Why the Crab Has No Head.* Minneapolis, MN: Carolrhoda, 1987.

Lessac, Frane. *My Little Island.* New York: Lippincott, 1984.

Lewin, Hugh. *Jafta's Father.* Minneapolis, MN: Carolrhoda, 1983.

———. *Jafta's Mother.* Minneapolis, MN: Carolrhoda, 1983.

———. *Jafta—and the Wedding.* Minneapolis, MN: Carolrhoda, 1983.

———. *Jafta—the Journey.* Minneapolis, MN: Carolrhoda, 1984.

———. *Jafta—the Town.* Minneapolis, MN: Carolrhoda, 1984.

———. *Jafta.* Minneapolis, MN: Carolrhoda, 1983.

Lexau, Joan. *Benjie.* New York: Dial, 1964.

———. *I Should Have Stayed in Bed.* New York: Harper & Row, 1965.

———. *Me Day.* New York: Dial, 1971.

———. *Stupid Ice Cream.* New York: Lippincott, 1968.

———. *The Rooftop Mystery.* New York: Harper & Row, 1968.

Lipsyte, Robert. *Free to Be Muhammad Ali.* New York: Harper & Row, 1978.

Little, Lessie, & Eloise Greenfield. *I Can Do It Myself.* New York: Crowell, 1978.

Lloyd, Errol. *Nini at Carnival* (Jamaica). New York: Crowell, 1978.

Lowery, Linda. *Martin Luther King Day.* Minneapolis, MN: Carolrhoda, 1987.

Martin, Patricia M. *The Little Brown Hen.* New York: Crowell, 1960.

McDermott, Gerald. *Anansi the Spider.* New York: Holt, 1972.

Musgrove, Margaret. *Ashanti to Zulu.* New York: Dial, 1973.

Pomerantz, Charlotte, & Franc Lessac. *The Chalk Doll.* New York: Lippincott, 1989.

San Souci, Robert D. *The Talking Eggs.* New York: Dial, 1989.

Schroeder, Alan. *Ragtime Tumpie.* Boston: Little, Brown, 1989.

Scott, Ann. *Sam.* New York: McGraw-Hill, 1967.

Seeger, Peter. *Abiyoyo.* New York: Macmillan, 1986.

Sherlock, Phillip. *Anansie, the Spider Man.* New York: Crowell, 1954.

Stanley, Diane, & Peter Vennema. *Shaka: A Zulu Tale.* New York: Morrow, 1988.

Steptoe, John. *Baby Says.* New York: Lothrop, 1988.

———. *Mufaro's Beautiful Daughters.* New York: Lothrop, 1987.

————. *My Special Best Words.* New York: Viking, 1974.

————. *Steve.* New York: Harper & Row, 1969.

Stock, Catherine. *Armien's Fishing Trip.* New York: Morrow, 1990.

Stolz, Mary. *Storm in the Night.* New York: Harper & Row, 1988.

Sutherland, E. *Playtime in Africa.* New York: Atheneum, 1962.

Thomas, Ianthe. *Hi, Mrs. Mallory.* New York: Harper & Row, 1979.

————. *Walk Home Tired Billy Jenkins.* New York: Harper & Row, 1974.

————. *Willie Blows a Mean Horn.* New York: Harper & Row, 1981.

Udry, Janice. *What Mary Jo Shared.* Niles, IL: Whitman, 1966.

Ward, Leila. *I Am Eyes—Ni Macbo.* New York: Scholastic, 1987.

Williams, Vera. *A Chair for My Mother.* New York: Greenwillow, 1982.

————. *Cherries and Cherries Pits.* New York: Greenwillow, 1986.

————. *More, More, More Said the Baby.* New York: Greenwillow, 1990.

————. *Something Special for Me.* New York: Greenwillow, 1983.

Winter, Jeanette. *Follow the Drinking Gourd.* New York: Knopf, 1988.

Yarbrough, Camille. *Cornrows.* New York: Putnam, 1979.

Young, Margaret E. *The Picture Life of Ralph J. Bunche.* New York: Watts, 1968.

Childrens Book's— Aging/Aged/Elderly

Aldridge, Josephine. *Fisherman's Luck.* New York: Parnassus, 1986.

Alexander, Martha. *The Story Grandmother Told.* New York: Dial, 1969.

Ardizzone, Edward. *Tim of the Lighthouse.* New York: Walck, 1968.

Baldwin, Anne E. *Sunflowers for Tina.* New York: Four Winds, 1978.

Bartoli, Jennifer. *Nonna.* New York: Harvey, 1975.

Blue, Rose. *Grandma Didn't Wave Back.* New York: Watts, 1972.

Borack, Barbara. *Grandpa.* New York: Harper, 1967.

Bulla, Clyde Robert. *The Sugar Pear Tree.* New York: Crowell, 1961.

Burningham, John. *Grandpa.* New York: Crowell, 1985.

Chorao, Kay. *Lester's Overnight.* New York: Dutton, 1977.

Constant, Helen. *The Gift.* New York: Knopf, 1983.

De Paola, Tomie. *Nana Upstairs and Nana Downstairs.* New York: Putnam, 1973.

————. *Now One Foot, Now the Other.* New York: Putnam, 1981.

————. *Watch Out for the Chicken Feet in Your Soup.* New York: Prentice-Hall, 1974.

Dobrin, Arnold. *Scat!* New York: Four Winds, 1971.

Fasslar, Joan. *My Grandpa Died Today.* New York: Hurnan Science Press, 198

Flora, James. *Grandpa's Farm.* New York: Harcourt Brace, 1965.

Gauch, Patricia Lee. *Grandpa & Me.* New York: McGann, 1972.

Goffstein, M. B. *Fish for Supper.* New York: Dial, 1976.

Goldman, Susan. *Grandma Is Somebody Special.* Niles, IL: Whitman, 1976.

————. *Grandpa and Me Together.* Niles, IL: Whitnan, 1978.

Greenfield, Eloise. *Grandmama's Joy.* New York: Collins, 1980.

————. *Grandpa's Face.* New York: Philomel, 1988.

Heins, Lucille. *My Very Special Friend.* New York: Judson, 1974.

Henriod, Lorraine. *Grandma's Wheelchair.* Niles, IL: Whitman, 1982.

Hoban, Russell. *How Tom Beat Captain Najork and His Hired Sportsman.* New York: Atheneum, 1974.

Jackson, Louise A. *Grandpa Had a Windmill, Grandma Had a Churn.* New York: Parent, 1977.

Kantrowitz, Mildred. *Maxie.* New York: Parent, 1970.

Kesselman, Wendy. *Emma.* Boston: Doubleday, 1980.

Lapp, Eleanor J. *The Mice Came Early This Year.* Niles, IL: Whitman, 1976.

Lasky, Kathryn. *I Have Four Names for Grandfather.* New York: Little, Brown, 1976.

Lexau, Joan M. *Benjie and His Own.* New York: Dial, 1970.

Loof, Jan. *My Granpa Is a Pirate.* New York: Harper & Row, 1968.

Lundgren, Max. *Matt's Grandfather.* New York: Putnam, 1972.

Mathis, Sharon Bell. *The Hundred Penny Box.* New York: Viking, 1975.

Miles, Miska. *Annie and The Old One.* New York: Little, Brown, 1971.

Montaufier, Poupa. *One Summer at Grandmother's House.* Minneapolis, MN: Carolrhoda, 1985.

Ness, Evaline. *Josefina February.* New York: Scribner's, 1963.

Newman, Shirley P. *Tell Me Grandpa, Tell Me Grandma.* New York: Houghton Mifflin, 1979.

Orr, Katherine. *My Grandpa and the Sea.* Minneapolis, MN: Carolrhoda, 1990.

Oxenburg, Helen. *Grandma & Grandpa.* New York: Dial, 1984.

Palay, Steven. *I Love My Grandma.* New York: Raintree, 1977.

Raynor, Dorka. *Grandparents Around the World.* Niles, IL: Whitman, 1977.

Schick, Eleanor. *Peter and Mr. Brandon.* New York: Macmillan, 1974.

Skorpen, Liesel Moak. *Mandy's Grandmother.* New York: Dial, 1975.

———. *Old Arthur.* New York: Dial, 1972.

Sleator, William. *The Angry Moon.* New York: Little, Brown, 1970.

Sonneborn, Ruth. *I Love Gram.* New York: Viking, 1971.

Thomas, Ianthe. *Hi, Mrs. Mallory.* New York: Harper & Row, 1979.

Tobias, Tobi. *Jane Wishing.* New York: Viking, 1977.

Udry, Janice May. *Mary Jo's Grandmother.* Niles, IL: Whitman, 1970.

Vigna, Judith. *Grandma Without Me.* Niles, IL. Whitman, 1984.

Whittman, Sally. *A Special Trade.* New York: Harper & Row, 1978.

Williams, Barbara. *Kevin's Grandma.* New York: Dutton, 1975.

Williams, Vera. *Music, Music for Everyone.* New York: Greenwillow, 1979.

Wood, Joyce. *Grandmother Lucy Goes on a Picnic.* New York: World, 1970.

Zolotow, Charlotte. *My Grandson Lew.* New York: Harper & Row, 1974.

Children's Books—Asian American

Ayer, Jacqueline. *NuDang and His Kite.* New York: Harcourt Brace, 1959.

Bang, Molly. *The Paper Crane.* New York: Greenwillow, 1985.

Bartosiak, Janet. *A Dog for Ramon.* New York: Dial, 1966.

Battes, Edith. *What Does the Rooster Say, Yoshio?* Niles, IL: Whitman, 1978.

Behrens, June. *Gung Hay Fat Choy:* Chicago: Children's Press, 1982.

Bishop, Claire. *The Five Chinese Brothers.* New York: Coward, 1938.

Bunting, Eve. *The Happy Funeral.* New York: Harper & Row, 1982.

Carpenter, Frances. *Tales of the Chinese Grandmother.* Boston: Doubleday, 1937.

Chang, Kathleen. *The Iron Moonhunter.* San Francisco: Children's Book Press, 1977.

Cheng Hou-tien. *Six Chinese Brothers.* New York: Holt, 1979.

Cheng Hou-tien. *The Chinese in New York.* New York: Holt, 1976.

Clark Ann Nolan. *In the Land of Small Dragon.* New York: Viking, 1979.

Coatsworth, E. *The Cat Who Went to Heaven.* New York: Macmillan, 1958.

Coer, Eleanor B. *Sadako and the Thousand Paper Cranes.* New York: Macmillan, 1979.

Coutant, Helen. *The First Snow.* New York: Knopf, 1974.

Demi. *Liang and the Magic Paintbrush.* New York: Harper & Row, 1982.

Epstein, Sam. *A Year of Japanese Festivals.* Easton, MD: Garrard, 1974.

———. *The Emperor's Plum Tree.* Easton, MD: Garrard, 1974.

Friedman, Ina R. *How My Parents Learned to Eat.* New York: Houghton Mifflin, 1984.

Hack, Marjorie. *The Story of Ping.* New York: Viking, 1933.

Handforth, T. *Mei-Li.* New York: Doubleday, 1938.

Hawkinson, L. *Dance, Dance Amy-Chan!* Niles, IL: Whitman, 1964.

Hong, Lily Toy. *How the Ox Star Fell from Heaven.* Niles, IL: Whitman, 1991.

Koopmans, Loek. *The Woodcutter's Mitten.* Brooklyn, NY: Crocodile Books, 1991.

Hidaho, Masako. *The Girl from the Snow Country.* New York: Kane/Miller, 1986.

Lattimore, E. *Little Pear, The Story of a Little Chinese Boy.* New York: Harcourt Brace, 1931.

Leaf, Margaret. *Eyes of the Dragon.* New York: Lothrop, 1987.

Lee, J. M. *Toad Is the Uncle of Heaven.* New York: Holt, Rinehart & Winston, 1985.

Lewis, Richard. *A Collection of Chinese and Japanese Poetry.* New York: Dial, 1964.

———. *In a Spring Garden.* New York: Dial, 1965.

———. *The Moment of Wonder.* New York: Dial, 1964.

Lewis, Thomas P. *The Dragon Kite.* New York: Holt, 1974.

Lifton, B. J. *The Cook and the Ghost Cat.* New York: Atheneum, 1965.

———. *The Dwarf Pine Tree.* New York: Atheneum, 1963.

Lobel, Arnold. *Ming-lo Moves the Mountain.* New York: Greenwillow, 1982.

Lord, Bette B. *In the Year of the Boar and Jackie Robinson.* New York: Harper & Row, 1978.

Louie, A. L. *Yeh Shen.* New York: Philomel, 1982.

Matsuno. *A Pair of Red Clogs.* New York: Collins, 1963.

Mauser, Pat. *A Bundle of Sticks.* New York: Atheneum, 1982.

McCunn, Ruthanne L. *Pie-Biter.* San Francisco: Design Ent, 1983.

———. *Thousand Pieces of Gold: A Biographical Novel.* Boston: Beacon Press, 1989.

McHugh, Elizabeth. *Raising a Mother Isn't Easy.* New York: Greenwillow, 1983.

McNair, Sylvia. *Korea.* Chicago: Children's Press, 1986.

Mosel, Arlene. *Tikki Tikki Tembo.* New York: Holt, 1968.

Nichols, Sally F. *Do You Not See: Sixteen Chinese Poems.* New York: Harper & Row, 1980.

Nitzaka, Kazuo. *Clouds.* Reading, MA: Addison-Wesley, 1975.

Pack, M. *Aekyung's Dream.* Chicago: Children's Press, 1978.

Paterson, Katherine. *Park's Quest.* New York: Dutton, 1988.

Pittman, Helena. *The Gift of the Willows.* Minneapolis, MN: Carolrhoda, 1988.

Politi, Leo. *Mieko.* New York: Golden Gates, 1969.

———. *Moy, Moy.* New York: Scribner's, 1960.

———. *Mr. Frog's Shop.* New York: Scribner's, 1979.

Saiki, Patsy Sumie. *Sachie, a Daughter of Hawaii.* Honolulu, HI: Kisaku, 1977.

Santa Elena, Antonio E. *Mahinhin: A Tale of the Philippines.* El Cerrito, CA: Downey Place, 1985.

Say, Allen. *Once Under the Cherry Blossom Tree.* New York: Harper & Row, 1974.

———. *The Bicycle Man.* New York: Houghton Mifflin, 1982.

Shute, Linda. *Momotano the Peach Boy.* New York: Lothrop, 1986.

Stock, Catherine. *Emma's Dragon Hunt.* New York: Lothrop, 1984.

Surat, Michelle Maria. *Angel Child, Dragon Child.* New York: Scholastic, 1983.

Takashima, Shizuye. *A Child in Prison Camp.* Pittsburgh, NY: Tundra Books of Northern New York, 1971.

Uchida, Yoshiko. *Journey Home.* New York: Atheneum, 1978.

———. *Journey to Topaz.* New York: Scribner's, 1971.

———. *Samurai of Gold Hill.* New York: Scribner's, 1972.

———. *Sumi and the Goat and the Tokyo Express.* New York: Scribner's, 1969.

———. *Sumi's Prize.* New York: Scribner's, 1964.

———. *The Best Bad Thing.* New York: Atheneum, 1983.

———. *The Birthday Visitor.* New York: Scribner's, 1975.

———. *The Happiest Ending.* New York: Atheneum, 1985.

———. *The Promised Year.* New York: Harcourt Brace, 1959.

———. *The Rooster Who Understood Japanese.* New York: Scribner's, 1976.

———. *The Forever Christmas Tree.* New York: Scribner's, 1963.

Waters, Kate, & Madeline Slovenz-Low. *Lion Dancer.* New York: Scholastic, 1990.

Watkins, Yako Kowashima. *So Far from the Bamboo Grove.* New York: Lothrop, 1986.

Wisniewski, David. *The Warrior and the Wise Man.* New York: Lothrop, 1989.

Wyndham, Robert. *Chinese Mother Goose Rhymes.* New York: Philomel, 1989.

Yashima, Mitsu, & Taro Yashima. *Momo's Kitten.* New York: Penguin, 1977.

Yashima, Taro. *Arrow Boy.* New York: Viking, 1955.

———. *Crow Boy,* New York: Penguin, 1976.

———. *Seashore Story.* New York: Viking, 1967.

———. *The Golden Footprints.* New York: World, 1960.

———. *The Village Tree.* New York: Viking, 1953.

———. *Umbrella.* New York: Viking, 1958.

Yolen, Jane. *The Emperor and the Kite.* New York: World, 1957.

———. *The Seeing Stick.* New York: Crowell, 1977.

Young, Ed. *Lon Po-Po.* New York: Philomel, 1989.

Ziner, Feenie. *Cricket Boy: A Chinese Tale Retold.* Boston: Doubleday, 1977.

Children's Books— Families

Adorjan, Carol. *That's What Friends Are For.* New York: Scholastic, 1990.

Bider, Djemma. *A Drop of Honey.* New York: Simon & Schuster, 1989.

Bourke, Linda. *Handmade ABC.* Boston: Addison-Wesley, 1981.

Drescher, Joan. *Your Family, My Family.* New York: Walker, 1980.

Elwin, Rosamund, & Michele Pause. *Asha's Mums.* Toronto: Women's Press, 1990.

Galloway, Priscilla. *Jennifer Has Two Daddies.* Toronto: Women's Press, 1985.

Hubley, John, & Penny Hubley. *A Family in Jamaica.* Minneapolis, MN: Lerner Publications, 1982.

Keats, Ezra Jack. *Peter's Chair.* New York: Harper & Row, 1967.

Leah, Michele, et al., *My Kind of Family: A Book for Kids in Single-Parent Homes.* Burlington, VT: Waterfront Books.

Lindsay, Jeanne Warren. *Do I Have a Daddy?* Buena Park, CA: Morning Glory Press, 1991.

Lloyd, Errol. *Nini at Carnival.* New York: Crowell, 1978.

Newman, Leslea. *Heather Has Two Mommies.* Boston: Alyson Wonderland, 1989.

———. *Gloria Goes to Gay Pride.* Boston: Alyson Wonderland, 1991.

Severance, Jane. *When Megan Went Away.* Carrboro, NC: Lollipop Power, 1979.

Simon, Norma. *All Kinds of Families.* Neil, IL: Whitman Albert, 1976.

———. *I Am Not a Crybaby.* New York: Puffin Books, 1989.

Sneve, Virginia Dancing Hawk. *Dancing Teepees: Poems of an Indian Youth.* New York: Holiday House, 1989.

Tax, Meredith. *Families.* Boston: Little, Brown, 1981.

Thomas, Marlo, & the Ms. Foundation. *Free to Be . . . A Family.* New York: McGraw-Hill, 1987.

Walter, Mildred Pitt. *Ty's One Man Band.* New York: Scholastic, 1980.

Willhoite, Michael. *Daddy's Roommate.* Boston: Alyson Wonderland, 1990

———. *Families.* Boston: Alyson Wonderland, 1991.

Children's Books—Gender Identity

Berenstain, Stan, & Jan Berenstain. *He Bear, She Bear.* New York: Random House, 1974.

Claffey, Anne. *Rapunzel's Revenge: Fairytales for Feminists.* Dublin, Ireland: Attic Press, 1985.

De Paola, Tomie. *Oliver Button Is a Sissy.* New York: Harcourt Brace Jovanovich, 1979.

Epstein, Vivian Sheldon. *ABC'S of What a Girl Can Be.* Denver, CO: VSE Publishers, 1980.

Homan, Dianne. *In Christina's Toolbox.* Durham, NC: Lollipop Power, 1981.

Mayer, Mercer. *There's Something in My Attic.* New York: Harper & Row, 1988.

Merriam, Eve. *Boys and Girls, Girls and Boys.* New York: Holt, Rinehart & Winston, 1972.

Merriam, Eve. *Mommies at Work.* New York: Simon & Schuster, 1989.

Miller, Deborah Uchill. *Modi in Motel.* Rockville, MD: Kar-Ben Copies, 1986.

Moche, Dinah L. *If You Were an Astronaut.* Racine, WI: Western Publishing Company, 1985.

Pogrebin, Letty Cottin, & The Ms. Foundation. *Stories for Free Children.* New York: McGraw-Hill, 1983.

Robbins, Sandra. *Big Annie.* New York: Shadow Box Theater Press, 1983.

Silverstein, Shel. *A Light in the Attic.* New York: Harper & Row, 1981.

Thomas, Marlo, & The Ms. Foundation. *Free to Be . . . You and Me.* New York: McGraw-Hill, 1974.

Zolotow, Charlotte. *William's Doll.* New York: Harper & Row, 1972.

Children's Books— Hispanic

Allyn, Paul. *The Picture Life of Herman Badillo.* New York: Watts, 1972.

Anderson, Eloise A. *Carlos Goes to School.* New York: Warner, 1973.

Aruego, Jose, & Aruego, Ariane. *A Crocodile Tale.* New York: Scholastic, 1972.

Atkinson, Mary. *Maria Teresa,* Carrboro, NC: Lollipop Power, 1979.

Balet, Jan. *The Fence.* New York: Delacorte, 1969.

Bannon, Laura. *Manuela's Birthday.* Niles, IL: Whitman, 1972.

Barth, Edna. *The Day Luis Was Lost.* New York: Little, Brown, 1971.

Baylor, Byrd. *Amigo.* New York: Macmillan, 1963.

Behn, Harry. *The Two Uncles of Pablo.* New York: Harcourt Brace, 1959.

Belpre, Pura. *Dance of the Animals.* New York: Warner, 1972.

———. *Juan Bobo and the Queen's Necklace.* New York: Warner, 1962.

———. *Once in Puerto Rico.* New York: Warner, 1973.

———. *Ote.* New York: Pantheon, 1969.

———. *Perez and Martina.* New York: Warner, 1961.

———. *Santiago.* New York: Warner, 1969.

———. *The Rainbow Colored Horse.* New York: Warner, l978.

———. *The Tiger and the Rabbit.* New York: Lippincott, 1965.

Blue, Rose. *I Am Here; Yo Estoy Aqui.* New York: Watts, 1971.

Bouchard, Lois. *The Boy Who Wouldn't Talk.* New York: Doubleday, 1969.

Brenner, Barbara. *Barto Takes the Subway.* New York: Knopf, 1962.

Brown, Tricia. *Hello Amigos!* New York: Holt, 1986.

Campion, Nardi. *Casa Means Home.* New York: Holt, 1970.

Colorado, Antonio J. *The First Book of Puerto Rico.* New York: Watts, 1978.

Cooney, Barbara. *Tortillas para Mama: Nursery Rhymes.* New York: Viking, 1981.

Delacre, Lulu. *Arroz con Leche: Popular Songs & Rhymes from Latin America.* New York: Scholastic, 1989.

De Paola, Tomie. *The Lady of Guadalupe.* New York: Holiday, 1980.

Ets, Marie Hall. *Gilberto and the Wind.* New York: Viking, 1963.

———. *Bad Boy, Good Boy.* New York: Crowell, 1967.

———. *Nine Days to Christmas.* New York: Viking, 1959.

Felt, Susan. *Rosa Too Little.* New York: Doubleday, 1950.

Forsee, Aylesa. *Too Much Dog.* New York: Lippincott, 1957.

Franchere, Ruth. *Cesar Chavez.* New York: Crowell, 1970.

Fulle, Suzanne. *Lanterns for Fiesta.* New York: Macrae, 1973.

Gates, Doris. *Blue Willow.* New York: Penguin, 1976.

Getz, Arthur. *Tar Beach.* New York: Dial, 1979.

Good, Loren. *Panchito.* New York: Coward, 1955.

Hack, Marjorie, & Karl Larrson. *Pedro.* New York: Macmillan, 1940.

Hazen, Nikki. *Grown-Ups Cry Too.* Carrboro, NC: Lollipop Power, 1973.

Keats, Ezra Jack. *My Dog Is Lost!* New York: Crowell, 1960.

Lewis, Thomas P. *Hill of Fire.* New York: Harper & Row, 1971.

Mann, Peggy. *The Street of Flower Boxes.* New York: Coward, 1966.

Martel, Cruz. *Yagua Days.* New York: Dial, 1976.

Maury, Inez. *My Mother the Mail Carrier; Mi Mama La Cartera,* trans. Norah Alemany. New York: Feminist Press, City University of New York, 1976.

Morrow, Elizabeth. *The Painted Pig.* New York: Knopf, 1930.

Paul, Paula. *You Can Hear a Magpie Smile.* New York: Nelson, 1980.

Politi, Leo. *Juanita.* New York: Scribner's, 1948.

———. *The Mission Bell.* New York: Scribner's, 1953.

———. *The Nicest Gift.* New York: Scribner's, 1973.

———. *Pedro, the Angel of Olvera Street.* New York: Scribner's, 1946.

———. *Rosa.* New York: Scribner's, 1963.

———. *Song of The Swallows.* New York: Macmillan, 1986.

———. *Three Stalks of Corn.* New York: Scribner's, 1978.

Prieto, Mariana. *Johnny Lost; Juanito Perdido.* New York: John Day, 1969.

Rosario, Idalia. *Idalia's Project ABC—Proyecto ABC: An Urban Alphabet Book in English and Spanish.* New York: Henry Holt, 1981.

Simon, Norma. *What Do I Do? Que Hago?* Niles, IL: Whitman, 1974.

Sonneborn, Ruth. *Friday Night Is Papa Night.* New York: Viking, 1970.

Stanek, Muriel. *I Speak English for My Mom.* Niles, IL: Whitman, 1989.

Talbot, Toby. *Coplas: Folk Poems in Spanish and English.* New York: Four Winds, 1972.

Todd, Barbara. *Juan Patricio.* New York: Putnam, 1972.

Wolf, Bernard. *In this Proud Land: The Story of a Mexican-American Family.* New York: Harper & Row, 1988.

Children's Books—Multicultural

Adler, David. *A Picture Book of Hanukkah.* New York: Holiday, 1982.

Aliki. *Mummies Made in Egypt.* New York: Crowell, 1977.

Allen, Pamela. *Who Sank the Boat?* New York: Coward, 1983.

Alonso, F. *La Gailina Paulina y el Grano de Trigo.* Santillana, Spain: Follett, 1975.

Anderson, Joy. *Jama and the Magic Jinn* (Arabic). New York: Lothrop, 1986.

Anno, Mitsumasa. *Anno's Britain.* New York: Philomel, 1982.

Aruego, Jose. *Rockabye Crocodile* (Filipino). New York: Greenwillow, 1988.

Babbitt, Ellen C. *The Jatakas, Tales of India.* New York: Appleton, 1940.

Baer, Edith. *This Is the Way We Go to School.* New York: Scholastic, 1990.

Beatty, Patricia. *Jonathan Down Under.* New York: Morrow, 1982.

Birrer, Cynthia, & William Birrer. *The Lady and the Unicorn* (French). New York: Lothrop, 1987.

Bonners, Susan. *Just in Passing.* New York: Morrow, 1989.

BrodMann, Aliana. *Such a Noise!* Brooklyn, NY: Kane/Miller, 1989.

Bunting, Eve. *The Big Red Barn.* New York: Harcourt Brace, 1979.

———. *How Many Days to America?* New York: Clarion, 1988.

Calhoun, Mary. *Jack and the Whoopee Wind.* New York: Morrow, 1987.

Cecil, Laura. *Listen to This.* New York: Greenwillow, 1987.

Cohen, Barbara. *Molly's Pilgrim* (Russian). New York: Lathrop, 1983.

De Armand, Dale. *Berry Woman's Children* (Eskimo). New York: Greenwillow, 1985.

De Paola, Tomie. *Big Anthony and the Magic Ring* (Italian). New York: Harcourt Brace, 1979.

———. *Strega Nonna.* Englewood Cliffs, NJ: Prentice-Hall, 1975.

———. *The Art Lesson.* Englewood Cliffs, NJ: Prentice-Hall, 1989.

———. *Tony's Bread* (Italian). New York: Whitebird, 1989.

Dooley, Norah. *Everybody Cooks Rice.* Minneapolis, MN: Carolrhoda, 1991.

Dorros, Arthur. *Tonight Is Carnival* (Peruvian). New York: Dutton, 1991.

Ganley, Helen. *Iyotie's Journey.* London: Deutsch, 1986.

Ginsburg, Mirra. *The Sun's Asleep Behind the Hill* (Armenian). New York: Greenwillow, 1982.

Greene, Carol. *Astria.* Chicago: Children's Press, 1986.

Haddithi, Mwenye. *Hot Hippo.* Boston: Little, Brown, 1986.

Harper, Anita. *How We Live.* New York: Harper & Row, 1977.

———. *How We Work.* New York: Harper & Row, 1977.

Haviland, Virginia. *Fairy Tales Told in Denmark.* New York: Little, Brown, 1971.

———. *Fairy Tales Told in Norway.* New York: Little, Brown, 1961.

———. *Fairy Tales Told in Italy.* New York: Little, Brown, 1965.

———. *Fairy Tales Told in Sweden.* New York: Little, Brown, 1966.

———. *Favorite Fairy Tales Told in France.* New York: Little, Brown, 1959.

Hirsch, Marilyn. *Potato Pancakes All Around: A Hanukkah Tale.* New York: Bonim, 1978.

———. *Ben Goes into Business.* New York: Holiday, 1973.

Hughes, Shirley. *Out and About.* New York: Lothrop, 1988.

Hutchins, Pat. *The Doorbell Rang.* New York: Greenwillow, 1986.

———. *The Wind Blew.* New York: Macmillan Children's Group, 1974.

Jonas, Ann. *The Quilt.* New York: Greenwillow, 1984.

Kaufman, Gita, & Curt Kaufman. *Hotel Boy.* New York: Atheneum, 1987.

———. *Rajesh.* New York: Atheneum, 1985.

Kipling, Rudyard. *Just So Stories.* Various editions and publishers.

———. *The Jungle Book.* Various editions and publishers.

Levine, Ellen. *I Hate English.* New York: Scholastic, 1982.

Little, Patricia. *Jack and Rosie.* New York: Greenwillow, 1989.

Lobel, Anita. *The Pancake* (Scandinavian). New York: Greenwillow, 1978.

Loh, Moray. *Tucking Mommy In.* New York: Orchard, 1988.

Mandelbaum, Pili. *You Be Me/I'll Be You.* Brooklyn, NY: Kane/Miller, 1990.

Maniche, Lise. *The Prince Who Knew His Fate* (Egyptian). New York: Philomel, 1982.

Martin, Bill. *Brown Bear, Brown Bear, What Do You See?* New York: Holt, 1983.

———. *Chicka Chicka Boom Boom.* New York: Simon & Schuster, 1989.

———. *I Am Freedom's Child.* Allen, TX: DLM, 1970.

Mikolaycak, Charles. *Babuska.* New York: Holiday, 1984.

Miller, Margaret. *Who Uses This?* New York: Greenwillow, 1990.

Mistral, Gabriela. *The Elephant and His Secret.* New York: Atheneum, 1974.

Morgan, Alison. *Paul's Kite.* New York: Atheneum, 1982.

Morris, Ann. *Bread, Bread, Bread.* New York: Lothrop, 1989.

———. *Hats, Hats, Hats.* New York: Lothrop, 1989.

———. *Loving.* New York: Lothrop, 1990.

———. *On the Go.* New York: Lothrop, 1990.

Nixon, Joan L. *The Gift* (Irish). New York: Macmillan, 1983.

Nordquist, Sven. *The Fox Hunt.* New York: Morrow, 1986.

Parcy, Florence Heide, & Judith Heide Gilliland. *The Day of Ahmed's Secret* (Egyptian). New York: Lothrop, 1990.

Phillips, Mildred. *The Sign on Mendel's Window.* New York: Macmillan, 1985.

Pomerantz, Charlotte. *The Mango Tooth.* New York: Greenwillow, 1977.

Rabe, Bernice. *The Balancing Girl.* New York: Dutton, 1981.

Rodahas, Kristina. *The Story of Wali Dad* (Indian). New York: Lothrop, 1988.

Rosenberg, M. *Living in Two Worlds.* New York: Lothrop, 1986.

Roth, Susan L. *The Story of Light.* New York: Morrow, 1990.

Ryder, Joanne. *Lizard in the Sun.* New York: Morrow, 1990.

Rynbach, Iris Van. *The Soup Stone.* New York: Greenwillow, 1988.

Schatz, Letta. *Benji's Magic Wheel.* Chicago: Follet, 1975.

Scott, Sally. *The Wonderful Beggars.* New York: Greenwillow, 1987.

Seuss, Dr. *The Sneetches.* New York: Random House, 1961.

Sonneborn, Ruth. *Seven in The Bed.* New York: Viking, 1968.

Spier, Peter. *People.* New York: Doubleday, 1980.

Stanley, Diane. *Fortune* (Persian). New York: Morrow, 1990.

Tashjian, Virginia A. *Three Apples from Heaven* (Middle Eastern). New York: Little, Brown, 1971.

Vagin, Vladirmnir, & Frank Asch. *Here Comes the Cat!* New York: Scholastic, 1989.

Walsh, Gill P. *Children of the Fox* (Greek). New York: Farrar, Straus & Giroux, 1978.

Weilerstein, Sadie. *The Best of K'tonton.* New York: Jewish Publication Society, 1960.

Williams, Karen Lynn. *Galimoto* (Malawi). New York: Lothrop, 1990.

Williams, Vera. *A Chair for My Mother.* New York: Greenwillow, 1982.

Wisniewski, David. *Elfwyn's Saga* (Viking). New York: Lothrop, 1990.

Yolen, Jane. *The Boy Who Had Wings* (Greek). New York: Crowell, 1974.

Zemach, Margot. *It Could Always Be Worse.* New York: Scholastic, 1976.

Children's Books—Native American

Aliki. *Corn Is Maize: The Gift of the Indians.* New York: Harper & Row, 1976.

Bales, Carol Ann. *Kevin Cloud: Chippewa Boy in the City.* Chicago: Reilly & Lee, 1972.

Batdorf, Carol. *Tinka: A Day in a Little Girl's Life.* Blaine, WA: Hancock House, 1990.

Baylor, Byrd. *Hawk i'm Your Brother.* New York: Scribner's, 1976.

————. *Moon Song.* New York: Scribner's, 1982.

————. *The Desert Is Theirs.* New York: Macmillan, 1986.

————. *They Put on Masks..* New York: Scribner's, 1975.

————. *When Clay Sings.* New York: Scribner's, 1972.

Benchley, Nathaniel. *Small Wolf.* New York: Harper & Row, 1972.

De Paola, Tomie. *The Legend of the Blue Bonnet.* New York: Putnam, 1983.

Garaway, Margaret K. *Ashkii and His Grandfather.* Tucson, AZ: Treasure Chest, 1989.

Goble, Paul. *The Gift of the Sacred Dog.* New York: Bradbury, 1980.

Goble, Paul, & Dorothy Goble. *The Girl Who Loved Wild Horses.* New York: Bradbury, 1975.

————. *Lone Bull's Horse Raid.* New York: Bradbury, 1973.

Greene, Carol. *Black Elk: A Man with a Vision.* Chicago: Children's Press, 1990.

Hale, Janet. *The Owl's Song.* New York: Avon, 1976.

Highwater, Jamake. *Moonsong Lullaby.* New York: Lothrop, 1981.

Martin, Bill, Jr., & John Archambault. *Knots on a Counting Rope.* Allen, TX: DLM, 1989.

————. *White Dynamite and Curly Kidd.* Allen, TX: DLM, 1983.

McDermott, Gerald. *Arrows to the Sun: A Pueblo Indian Tale.* New York: Viking, 1974.

McNutt, Nan. *The Button Blanket.* Acme, MI: Workshop Publications, 1989.

Monjo, F. N. *Indian Summer.* New York: Harper & Row, 1968.

Peyton, John L. *Voices from the Ice.* Newark, OH: McDonald & Woodward, 1990.

Roland, Donna. *Grandfather's Stories.* San Diego, CA: Open My World, 1991.

————. *More of Grandfather's Stories.* San Diego, CA: Open My World, 1991.

Searcy, Margaret Z. *Wolf Dog of the Woodland Indians.* Gretna, LA: Pelican, 1991.

Shemie, Bonnie. *Houses of Bark, Tipi Wigwam, & Longhouse.* Plattsburgh, NY: Tundra Books of Northern New York, 1990.

Sneve, Virginia Driving Hawk. *Dancing Teepees: Poems of an Indian Youth.* New York: Holiday House, 1989.

Steptoe, John. *The Story of the Jumping Mouse.* New York: Lothrop, 1984.

Talaswaima, Terrance. *The Eagle Hunt.* Oraibi, AZ: Hopi, 1974.

Waterton, Betty. *A Salmon for Simon.* New York: Atheneum, 1981.

Children's Books— Physically Challenged

Arthur, Ruth. *Portrait of Margarita.* New York: Atheneum, 1968.

Aseltine, L., & E. Mueller. *I'm Deaf and It's Okay.* Niles, IL: Whitman, 1986.

Brown, Tricia. *Someone Special, Just Like You.* New York: Holt, 1984.

Charlip, Remy, et al. *An ABC of Finger Spelling and Sign Language.* New York: Parents, 1974.

Fassler, Joan. *Don't Worry Dear.* New York: Human Sciences, Whitman, 1971.

———. *Howie Helps Himself.* Niles, IL: Whitman, 1975.

———. *One Little Girl.* New York: Human Sciences, 1969.

Greenfield, Eloise. *Darlene.* New York: Methuen, 1980.

Heide, Florence. *Sound of Sunshine, Sound of Rain.* New York: Parents, 1972.

Jensen, Virginia, & Dorca Haller. *What's That?* New York: World, 1977.

Lasker, Joe. *He's My Brother.* Niles, IL: Whitman, 1974.

L'Engle, Madeline. *The Young Unicorns.* New York: Farrar, Straus & Giroux, 1968.

Litchfield, A. *A Button in Her Ear.* Niles, IL: Whitman, 1976.

———. *A Cane in Her Hand.* Niles, IL: Whitman, 1977.

———. *Words in Our Hands.* Niles, IL: Whitman, 1980.

Little, Jean. *Mine for Keeps.* New York: Little, 1962.

Maher, Ramona. *The Blind Boy and the Loon and Other Eskimo Myths.* New York: Day, 1969.

Platt, Kim. *Hey, Dummy.* New York: Dell, 1971.

Power, Mary Ellen. *Our Teacher's in a Wheelchair.* Niles, IL: Whitman, 1986.

Raskin, Ellen. *Spectacles.* New York: Atheneum, 1978.

Stanek, Muriel. *Left, Right; Left Right!* Niles, IL: Whitman, 1969.

Sullivan, Mary Beth, & Linda Bourke. *A Show of Hands.* New York: Scholastic, 1980.

Thomas, William. *The New Boy Is Blind.* New York: Thomas, 1980.

Wojciechowska, Maia. *A Sing Light.* New York: Bantam, 1968.

Wolf, Bernard. *Don't Feel Sorry for Paul.* New York: Lippincott, 1974.

Parent Resources— Self-Esteem

Clemens, Harris, & Reynold Bean. *How to Discipline Children Without Feeling Guilty.* Los Angeles: Price Stern Sloan, 1978, 1990.

———. *How to Teach Children Responsibility.* Los Angeles: Price Stern Sloan, 1978, 1990.

Dinkmeyer, Don, & Gary D. McKay. *Raising a Responsible Child.* New York: Simon & Schuster, 1973.

Gordon, Thomas. *Teaching Children Self-Discipline . . . at Home and at School: New Ways for Parents and Teachers to Build Self-Control, Self-Esteem, and Self-Reliance.* New York: Time Books, 1989.

Marston, Stephanie. *The Magic of Encouragement: Nurturing Your Child's Self-Esteem.* New York: Morrow, 1990.

Nelson, Jane. *Positive Discipline.* Fair Oaks, CA: Sunrise Press, 1981.

Organizational Resources

National Council for Self-Esteem, P.O. Box 277877, Sacramento, CA 95827. A national membership organization dedicated to promoting the development of self-esteem and personal responsibility in schools. Write for a free newsletter and application form.

Siccone Institute, 2151 Union Street, San Francisco, CA 94123. Offers training and consulting services in the areas of education, business, and personal development. Inservice workshops are available for administrators, teachers, students, and parents in areas including educational leadership, self-esteem and responsibility, communication and teamwork, and teacher as coach.